Warwick at War
1939–45

This book is dedicated to all those Warwickians who fought on land, sea and in the air, and also to their friends and families who carried on the fight at home.

Warwick at War
1939–45

Graham Sutherland

PEN & SWORD
HISTORY

AN IMPRINT OF PEN & SWORD BOOKS LTD.
YORKSHIRE – PHILADELPHIA

First published in Great Britain in 2020 by
Pen & Sword Military
An imprint of
Pen & Sword Books Ltd
Yorkshire – Philadelphia

ISBN 978 1 52672 2 355

A CIP catalogue record for this book is
available from the British Library.

Printed and bound in England by TJ International Ltd, Padstow, Cornwall

Pen & Sword Books Limited incorporates the imprints of Atlas, Archaeology,
Aviation, Discovery, Family History, Fiction, History, Maritime, Military,
Military Classics, Politics, Select, Transport, True Crime, Air World,
Frontline Publishing, Leo Cooper, Remember When, Seaforth Publishing,
The Praetorian Press, Wharncliffe Local History, Wharncliffe Transport,
Wharncliffe True Crime and White Owl.

For a complete list of Pen & Sword titles please contact

PEN & SWORD BOOKS LIMITED
47 Church Street, Barnsley, South Yorkshire, S70 2AS, England
E-mail: enquiries@pen-and-sword.co.uk
Website: www.pen-and-sword.co.uk

Or

PEN AND SWORD BOOKS
1950 Lawrence Rd, Havertown, PA 19083, USA
E-mail: Uspen-and-sword@casematepublishers.com
Website: www.penandswordbooks.com

Contents

Introduction

Warwick at War 1939–45 is not a history of the Second World War: it is an account of how this catastrophic event affected the county town of Warwick and its inhabitants.

In late September 1938, what became known as the Munich Crisis came to a head concerning the fate of Germans who lived in parts of Europe other than Germany. British Prime Minister Neville Chamberlain, well remembered for his phrase 'Peace in our time', has long since been regarded by many as an appeaser to Hitler. Originally considered by many to be a hero, that view quickly changed when it became apparent that Hitler had no intention of abiding by the so-called agreement. Yet it can be argued his Munich Agreement bought us another twelve months' breathing space to prepare for an inevitable war.

What is not quite so well-known is that Britain had been preparing for war before the Munich Agreement, despite a reluctance in many places to face facts. Wartime exercises were held half-heartedly, with a noticeable lack of funding and equipment. It seemed to be a case of having to do it because it was so decreed, but that was as far as it went: lip service only and at the minimum of cost and inconvenience.

It was also something of an eye-opener for many. While wars tend to make everyone pull together, there would always be those who had their eyes on any chance to make money. Granted, they would be more prevalent in larger towns and cities and not so much in places like Warwick, but there were those who had built up their own little empires at work and were far from happy with the disruption that a war would bring to them.

When compared to places such as nearby Coventry, Warwick was only bombed and strafed once. However, this relief meant a large influx of refugees and evacuees who brought their own problems with them to Warwick.

When looking at life in Warwick during this period, the reader should remember that what happened here also occurred in other parts of the country. What happened on the war fronts also affected people left at home who had family and friends on active service with all the heartbreak that might bring. The country struggled to carry on as near normally as possible.

Main Participants

The Allied Powers:

Great Britain, USA (from December 1941), Soviet Union (from June 1941), China, France, India, Canada, Australia, New Zealand, South Africa, Italy (from 1943).

The Axis Powers:

Germany, Italy (until 1943), Japan, Romania, Bulgaria, Hungary.

Notes

1) Where words are followed by capitalized abbreviations in parentheses, those acronyms will be used thereafter. An example would be the Royal Warwickshire Regiment (RWR).

2) Any comments/explanations made by the author will be shown in brackets. For example, [the author lived here as a child].

3) Warwick inhabitants will be referred to as Warwickians.

4) All addresses, unless stated otherwise, are in Warwick.

5) St Nicholas Park is the Park.

6) Churches are referenced by their names; e.g. St Mary's, not St Mary's Collegiate Church.

7) Market Place and Market Square are referred to as the Square.

8) Each chapter examines the day-to-day private and public issues affecting Warwickians during this period, sometimes influenced by events happening abroad. Many things we take for granted today were very different eighty years ago. Despite its various problems, our National Health Service allows us free access to doctors and other medical services. This was not the case in 1939 and someone other than the State had to pay for such treatment; the exception being members of the armed forces.

Conversion Tables

(NB: It is not always possible to convert the old to the new exactly. Consequently, each figure has been rounded up to its nearest modern-day equivalent. For today's values, multiply by 60.)

Currency:

Sterling	Decimal	Sterling	Decimal
1/4d	01p	5s	25p
3/4d	01p	6s	30p
1d	01p	7s	35p
2d	01p	8s	40p
3d	01p	9s	45p
4d	02p	10s	50p
5d	02p	11s	55p
6d	03p	12s	60p
7d	03p	13s	65p
8d	04p	14s	70p
9d	04p	15s	75p
10d	04p	16s	80p
11d	05p	17s	85p
1s	05p	18s	90p
2s	10p	19s	95p
3s	15p	20s	100p
4s	20p		

Weight:

Avoirdupois	Decimal
16 ounces (oz) = 1lb	.45 kilogram (kg)
14 pounds (lb) = 1 stone	6.35kg
28lb = 1 quarter (qtr)	12.7kg
4 qtr = 1 hundredweight (cwt)	50.8kg
20 cwt = 1 ton	1,016kg

Distance:

Imperial	Decimal
1 inch	2.54cms
12 inches = 1 foot	30.48cms
3 feet = 1 yard	91.44cms
1760 yard = 1 mile	1.61km

Military Medal Glossary during 1939-45. (Some classifications were changed in 1993).

NOTE: All the below awards include former members of the Commonwealth

DFC   Distinguished Flying Cross awarded to commissioned RAF officers, for acts of valour and devotion to duty when flying. In 1941 included Fleet Air Arm officers.

DSC   Distinguished Service Cross awarded to Royal Navy and other Services for example of bravery.

DSM   Distinguished Service Medal awarded to members of the Royal Navy up to and including chief petty officers for bravery and resourcefulness on active service at sea.

DSO   Distinguished Service Order awarded to officers for distinguished service in wartime especially in armed combat.

MC   Military Cross awarded to commissioned officers for exemplary gallantry during military operations.

MM   Military Medal same as Military Cross but for non-commissioned personnel.

OBE   Order of the British Empire awarded to civil and military personnel for gallantry and public service.

VC   Victoria Cross is the highest and most prestigious military award for gallantry in the face of the enemy.

CHAPTER ONE

A Brief History of Warwick

Warwick's origins as a town began in the year 914AD, when Ethelfleda, daughter of Alfred the Great, came to the area. She and her husband were determined to sort out the troublesome Danes, which they did.

Whilst she was the founder of the town, Warwick's origins go back some 5,000 years to when it was a small settlement by the River Avon (Avon). It was originally thought that there had been

Warwick Town Crest. (Author's collection)

Ethelfleda plaque in Castle Street. (Author's collection)

little Roman activity in the area, but this belief changed early in 2018 when the foundations of a large and prosperous villa were discovered off the Banbury Road.

Sadly the town could not celebrate its millennium in 1914 because the country was then at war with Germany. Now, in 1939, only twenty-five years later, we were once more at war, this time with Nazi Germany.

Over time, Warwick has enjoyed a varied history as a market and county town, but with many changes in recent years. Although Ethelfleda began the castle, significant changes were implemented during the following centuries, with a gradual move from it being a defensive building to a country house.

Various Earls of Warwick played important parts throughout England's history and not all of them died peacefully. For instance, Richard Neville, also known as 'Warwick the Kingmaker', was killed at the Battle of Barnet in 1471. Another earl was Lady Jane Grey's father-in-law, who was executed for treason by Queen Mary. We should not forget another earl who was killed at Lichfield in 1643 fighting against Charles I. One of the more controversial earls was Richard Beauchamp who won fame, or possibly infamy, through his role in the ultimate trial and execution of Joan of Arc in 1431. Some argue that he was a war hero, but others think the term war criminal is more appropriate.

The early eighteenth-century buildings, particularly in the High Street and Jury Street, along with the magnificent St Mary's Collegiate Church, owe their creation to the rebuilding of the town following the disastrous fire of 1694. Fortunately, the wonderful Beauchamp Chapel in St Mary's, created by Richard Beauchamp who is buried there, was one of the few parts of the old church to survive the fire.

He is buried in a magnificent tomb that takes centre stage in the chapel. His effigy is lying on its back with hands clasped as if in prayer. Follow his eyes: they are looking at a picture of the Virgin Mary in the chapel's ceiling. Is he is asking for forgiveness?

Alongside him is the tomb of Robert Dudley, Earl of Leycester [his spelling], and long-time friend of Queen Elizabeth I. They never married and after the suspicious death of his first wife, Amy Robsart, Dudley married Lettice Knollys. She outlived him by many years and they are buried together, with her effigy on the tomb being higher than his!

Dudley gave his name to the Lord Leycester Hospital, which is Warwick's most iconic building and situated by the Westgate entrance into the town. Despite its name, the building is not a medical hospital but was acquired by Dudley to house some of his retired military retainers and is still used for such purposes.

Other earls have been responsible for ensuring that they controlled Warwick, both at local and general elections, always taking care to blame their agents for any wrongdoings such as bribery, threats, etc. More recently, their growing financial

Robert Dudley, founder of the Lord Leycester Hospital. (Public domain)

problems resulted in the castle being sold. Today (2020), it is part of the Merlin Entertainments Group.

Until the 1970s, Budbrooke Barracks, just outside Warwick, were home to the Royal Warwickshire Regiment (RWR) whose origins go back to 1685. Sadly, the regiment no longer exists, although its museum remains in the town, at least for the moment (2020). The former barracks site is now part of the new village of Hampton Magna.

The other main military connection is the Warwickshire Yeomanry, now merged with the Worcestershire Yeomanry. Along with the RWR, they fought with distinction in the First World War and took part in the last unsupported cavalry charge in military history at the Battle of Huj in 1917. They maintain an excellent museum at Warwick Court House.

Royal Warwickshire Regiment antelope cap badge. (Author's collection)

B Squadron Warwickshire Yeomanry in the Middle East, 1940. (Warwickshire Yeomanry Museum Trust)

Old courts in Northgate Street. (Author's collection)

During the eighteenth and nineteenth centuries, Warwick was a busy road and canal transport centre with its accompanying trade.

Warwick lost its borough status in 1974 and became part of Warwick District Council (WDC), whose headquarters are in neighbouring Royal Leamington Spa (Leamington). Warwick Town Council, called Warwick Borough Council (WBC) in this book, still exists, albeit with limited powers and budgets. Warwick lost its crown and magistrates' courts, police and fire stations to Leamington, but still retains the headquarters of Warwickshire County Council (WCC). To be fair, the building which once housed the Quarter Sessions, Assizes and later Crown Courts was fine in the pre-computer and VDU age, but sadly proved unsuitable and inadequate for today's technology.

Warwick has expanded dramatically since 1945 and continues to do so. Since the 1970s, Woodloes Park, Warwick Gates and Chase Meadow housing developments have been built and more are planned.

CHAPTER TWO

The Road to War: 1919–39

It was once believed that the Second World War was inadvertently caused by a man from nearby Leamington: Henry Tandy or Tandey. As a private soldier in the First World War, he had two claims to fame: the first when he won the Victoria Cross; the second much more controversial. Allegedly he saved the life of a certain Adolf Hitler when he could have killed him, but

Private Henry Tandy (or Tandey) VC. (Duke of Wellington's Regimental Museum)

there is some speculation today as to the truth of this story. We know that Hitler served in the First World War and had he not survived it, the course of history could have been very different.

Along with many Germans, Hitler felt that his country had been humiliated by the Treaty of Versailles which was signed on 28 June 1919. The terms were harsh and not lessened by Germany's delays in agreeing to the final treaty. Hitler then wasted no time in doing something about it.

By 29 July 1921, he was leader of the National Socialist Party: the Nazis. In the following years they grew in popularity and became the second-largest political party in Germany. Hitler became Chancellor on 30 January 1933, and the first concentration camp soon appeared. He acquired dictatorial powers and wasted no time in using them.

The 1930s have been referred to as 'the Age of Anxiety' as people watched Hitler's activities.

Treaty of Versailles, 1919. (Bundesarchiv bild)

In August 1934, he became the Führer of Germany. Jews were persecuted, and the Gestapo secret police operated outside the law. On 16 March 1935, Hitler began military conscription, expressly forbidden by the Treaty of Versailles. In 1936 the Spanish Civil War began, with Germany and Italy supporting Franco's Nationalist Party. Germany and Italy signed the Rome-Berlin Axis Agreement. Some of these new troops fought in the Spanish Civil War, using this valuable battle experience to their advantage in the forthcoming conflict.

Despite Hitler's actions at home and abroad, world leaders were reluctant to recognize the threat he posed or do anything about it. He had many friends in Britain, America and elsewhere. However, opinions started to change in 1938 and war with Germany seemed inevitable.

On 30 September 1938, Prime Minister Neville Chamberlain achieved what he claimed was 'peace in our time' following a meeting with Hitler, Mussolini and French President Daladier.

Many pictures show Chamberlain returning home waving his piece of paper, which Hitler had signed and claimed peace in our time. It was soon apparent, however, that Hitler's promise was not worth the paper it was written on and war was coming.

Chamberlain was criticized for his so-called appeasement with Germany, but it gave Britain several more valuable months to prepare for war, although many opposed such plans as being provocative.

Marshal Ferdinand Foch of the French army was a far-sighted man, who argued for even harsher treatment of his former enemies before the Treaty of Versailles was signed. However, nobody listened to him and he faded from the public eye. Yet his comments after the signing should not be forgotten: 'This is not peace. It is an armistice for twenty years.'

By August 1939, Robert Anthony Eden, Warwick's MP, described the international situation as 'anxious and menacing'. He wanted peace but not appeasement. An astute individual, Eden realized that only force would stop Hitler. Soon after war was declared, he became Minister for Dominion Affairs and later the Secretary of State for War.

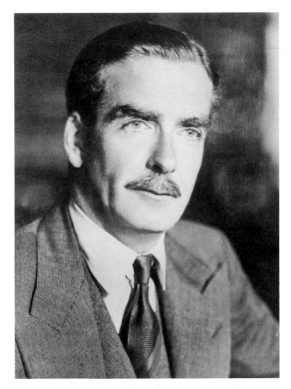

Robert Anthony Eden MP. (Public domain)

The Second World War began on Sunday, 3 September 1939, just twenty years and sixty-five days after Foch's comments.

Whatever the rights and wrongs of Chamberlain's piece of paper, it gained the country some valuable time to prepare for war. Although memories of the First World War were very much alive, it was quickly realized how this war would be very different. Between 1914 and 1918, most of the fighting had been on land or at sea, with a few scattered attacks on Britain from the air. Being an island, we had not been conquered or occupied by enemy powers since the year 1066. During the First World War, there had been few civilian casualties. That was all about to change in the looming conflict.

Undoubtedly the fighting at home would come from the skies and its accompanying devastation, as witnessed during the

Spanish Civil War: the protection afforded by our island status no longer applied. The civilian population would be involved, and heavy casualties were inevitable. Whoever controlled the skies would ultimately win the war.

Even before Munich, some influential people realized that time was running out and preparations needed to be made. On 1 April 1935 the Home Office Air Raid Precautions (ARP) Department was created, although government concern about air attacks had first arisen in 1924.

However, such preparations and defence schemes could only reduce the risks from air-raids, not stop them. After 1938, protective equipment was the responsibility of local authorities

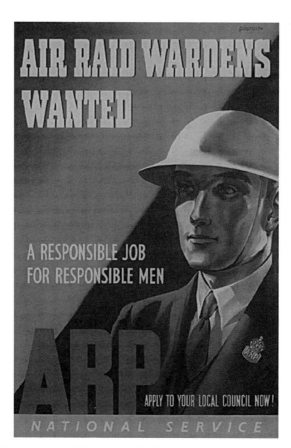

Air-Raid Precautions (ARP) poster. (Public domain)

and the police to provide. It was an inexact science which altered as circumstances demanded.

Not all these arrangements worked smoothly. Many organizations, including local authorities, believed they were unnecessary. Smaller towns objected to spending the money, but who would be blamed if the town did nothing and was later bombed? Without legal requirements to provide these services, some authorities would have done nothing.

Post-Munich, the government prepared for war. It was the worst-case scenario which everyone had hoped would never happen, but the threat could not be ignored.

How would the country cope?

CHAPTER THREE

Setting the Scene: 1939–45

Children

In wartime, everyone is affected to some degree. Life continued but as time progressed, changes were made as events happened. It was a mainly trouble-free existence for many children. Air-raids took place, which affected not just the specific targets but other areas not directly bombed. The government's primary home objective was to minimize the death toll caused by bombing, and the survival of children was particularly important. The country depended on them for the future.

Many children found the war was a huge adventure. Granted, it was not so enjoyable in heavily-bombed areas from where evacuations took place. Life was interrupted and sometimes children were aware of friends not being seen any more, possibly having been evacuated or even killed. Few children complained about school being interrupted. Regular education was not fully restored until after 1945. A shortage of teachers did not help. Children helped the war effort by collecting newspapers, wild fruit, acting as messengers and raising money for numerous causes, in addition to collecting shrapnel.

For youngsters brought up in this environment, it was the only life they knew. Fathers became distant figures and children were in the sole charge of their mothers. The author remembers how whenever his father came home, the latter had the full attention of his mother and yours truly was relegated to second place. This 'intrusion' rankled following demobilization and could become a serious problem for many fathers and their younger children. The older ones understood more and had missed their absent fathers. Along with their mothers, they worried about receiving the dreaded telegram informing of his being 'Killed in Action'. Telegrams which merely recorded a man as missing held out more hope, albeit often a forlorn one.

Profiteers made money and children were not excluded from this. In late 1944, the Board of Trade warned mothers not to buy expensive but poor-quality Christmas presents of wooden bricks for 9s a box.

The arrival of the first evacuee children brought an unforeseen problem with them. It was the end of the school holidays and they had not been checked for nits (head lice) for several weeks. This meant extra work for the nit nurses. WCC helped with their schooling.

Communications

A well-known saying is 'the first casualty of war is truth'. Rumours prevailed, aided by Nazi sympathizers such as William Joyce alias Lord Haw-Haw. He would regularly broadcast on the radio, giving out a wide variety of false information about what was happening in Britain. Today we call it 'fake news'. Misinformation is nothing new; only how it is spread. People who knew the truth about his reports of death and destruction were amused, but their loved ones many miles from home might be concerned. It was psychological warfare. Joyce was hanged after the war.

Regardless of the methods used, communications were disrupted by enemy activity. Some methods were innovative and adapted to the circumstances. Most people owned a radio, or wireless as it was then called. The news bulletins were vital to inform them what was happening, albeit within the parameters of censorship. Television was such a rarity as to be discounted.

Laughable though it may seem today, pigeons were a valuable means of communication, albeit with no 100 per cent guarantee of success. Approximately 250,000 pigeons were used at home and abroad. There was no forced conscription of pigeons, but

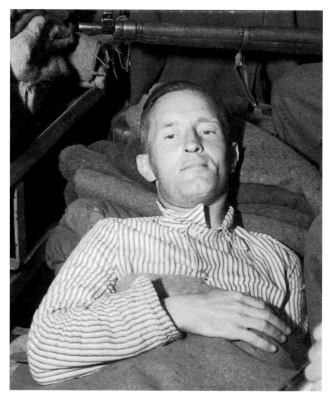

William Joyce, alias Lord Haw-Haw. (Public domain)

fanciers who did not volunteer their birds suddenly found that they no longer received any corn with which to feed them. It was an offence to kill homing pigeons. The RAF wanted people to report anyone who did so. When a dead bird was found with a message container attached, it was taken to the police. If the container was blue with a white patch, it was to be opened and the enclosed instructions followed. Later, pigeons went on air-raids. If the plane was shot down in the sea, the co-ordinates would be attached to the pigeon, hoping it could convey the information back to base.

Radio was also a morale-booster, especially if there was little good news. Even during the blitz, the news never stopped. *Music While You Work* was a great comfort to struggling housewives and a great-spirit raiser for factory workers. Dame Vera Lynn was not just 'the Forces' Sweetheart' but also very much in demand on the home front. Laughter was encouraged.

The radio played an important part in youngsters' lives, and the BBC's *Children's Hour* from 5.00 pm to 6.00 pm was very popular. So was its presenter, Derek McCulloch, known as Uncle Mac. The programme started in 1922 and ended in 1964. The author remembers it in the post-war years and Uncle Mac's farewell at the end of each programme: 'Good night children, everywhere.'

Another offshoot on the radio was the BBC Forces Programme created for service personnel but this soon became the nation's favourite.

Sims radio. (David Unitt)

Defensive Measures

What could be done to oppose a possible invasion? Latter-day experts contend it would have been a swift victory for the Germans, although their advance would be made as difficult as possible.

Uniformed enemy were obvious, but who else could be trusted? With few or no regular troops available, much of the country's defence would be left to older and less physically fit men and women, including an English Resistance Organization. We shall never know what they would have achieved. Armchair critics are scathing many years later, but they were all that was available and plans were made. In the absence of manufactured weapons, improvised ones would suffice, such as booby traps and Molotov cocktails (home-made fire bombs in bottles). Old wartime concrete defensive positions known as pill boxes can still be seen today.

Food

Despite rationing, extra food was often more available in the countryside than in the towns. Fish was not rationed but became expensive as the navy commandeered many fishing vessels. Other fish such as snoek [pronounced snook] and whale meat were never popular. Bread was never rationed but only sold when it was at least a day old, hopefully discouraging too much being eaten. It worked, and the bread was disliked and nicknamed 'Hitler's secret weapon'. Many commodities were not rationed but scarce which led to queuing. One of the better-known bakers in Warwick and Leamington was Sensicles who had a 1st Grade Diploma and also sold milk. Their bread was available at Berry's in Emscote Road, Carter's in Paradise Street and Harris's in Peel Road.

School dinners were started to help working parents if their children did not go home at lunchtime. Warwick school dinners were all cooked at the former Central Hospital at Hatton and delivered in insulated containers by Mr Farand driving a Humber Snipe. There were never any chips, and whale meat was often used in stews. Spam came later. Graham Doughty described them as 'Absolutely bloody fantastic' and 'Brilliant'.

Health

Regardless of the war, people continued living and dying, but the war put an added burden on the medical facilities. There was no National Health Service and non-war-related treatment was not free: someone had to pay for it.

Home Defence

ARP

It was hoped that air-raids would never happen, but they did. Although Warwick was never a prime target, this situation could always change, especially given the town's proximity to Coventry. The Baedeker raids during April and May 1942 proved this point, when the Luftwaffe bombed non-military targets such as King's Lynn and Bath. The objective was to bomb every place which appeared with three stars in the Baedeker tourist guide. They were unsuccessful, but made otherwise 'safe' areas think again.

The main task for the defenders was to destroy the bombers before they dropped their loads. Realistically this could never happen, but the raiders received heavy fire from the ground and suffered casualties. A similar situation existed in the Axis countries. Sorties (flights) from Germany had a limited range, but this changed following the fall of France.

Britain's great advantage was the Radio Detection and Ranging (RADAR) system, which was crucial during the Battle of Britain (this acronym was coined by the US navy). Radar enabled German aircraft to be spotted and targeted before they left France. Nevertheless, 60,595 British civilians were killed during air-raids.

Protection on the home front was left to volunteers such as Air Raid Precautions (ARP) wardens because the military had other priorities. The first essential was to provide some type of defence measures to protect people from air-raids. Help would be provided, wherever possible, by the police, although it was anticipated that this might be minimal. The wardens' duties included enforcing blackout regulations; sounding air-raid sirens; issuing gas masks; guiding people to public shelters; rescuing people; cordoning off unexploded bombs; and reporting incidents such as fires, etc. Information and intelligence control centres were planned.

Some 80 per cent of all ARP staff were unpaid and acted for patriotic reasons. Volunteers had to be at least 30 years old, and one-sixth of them were women. They were shabbily treated. The author had an aunt, Jessie Ruddock, who was a warden in Dartford, Kent. The war was almost two months old before they received their equipment and they waited another year for their overalls. Some government official decided that uniforms were unnecessary until May 1941. These were a dark blue battledress and beret for the men, and a similar-coloured four-pocket tunic and skirt for the women. In another parsimonious move, wardens were issued with cheaper helmets with holes drilled in them, indicating that they were not for front-line use. They received a fortnightly ration of ½ oz of tea, 1 oz of sugar and two biscuits. Home Office workers had ham and eggs; egg and chips; tea and coffee. 1,355 wardens were killed while on duty.

Deep air-raid shelters were discouraged by the government who were worried about a defeatist attitude with added health and sanitary problems. Public shelters were intended only for people who could not get home in time. WBC estimated that each public shelter would cost £100 to create.

The wealthy had their own private shelters. As the war progressed, cheaper options appeared. One was the Anderson shelter, holding up to six people, which was delivered free to families earning less than £250 per annum and at a cost of £7 for others. It comprised two curved walls of corrugated metal, which were bolted together and set into the ground. While good for deflecting blast, being in the ground caused cold, damp and sometimes flooding. Another option was the indoor Morrison shelter which was a reinforced table caged with wire mesh

ARP Mrs Jessie Ruddock. (Author's collection)

surrounds to prevent injury from flying debris. It was quick, easy to use and cheaper. Alternatively, house-owners dug a trench in the garden or sat out raids under the stairs. Air-raid sirens were a matter for local authorities when it came to their siting and testing.

Blackout

Blackout regulations came into force on 1 September 1939 and required all windows and doors to be covered to prevent any indoor light being visible from outside. Night-time bombing was a real threat and the idea was to prevent any lights guiding bombers. It was most unpopular, and many doubted its effectiveness. Similar doubts had existed during the First World War. The government erroneously warned how a lit cigarette could be seen from 20,000ft above by enemy aircraft. The Luftwaffe used other means of navigating to their target. St Mary's in Warwick was reputedly a landmark for aircraft attacking Coventry.

Street lights, motor vehicle lights and bicycle lamps were included in these precautions, quickly becoming a nightmare for road users and leading to a sharp rise in fatal collisions. Those most at risk were pedestrians followed by drivers, especially between 10.00 pm and 11.00 pm. Some relaxation and dim lights were permitted at dangerous junctions. Approximately one person in five received an injury in the blackout. By October 1939,

Blackout regulations. (Public domain)

pedestrians could use hand torches, provided they were covered in two layers of material and switched off during a raid.

The Civil Defence (CD) Service was another voluntary non-military organization established by the Home Office in 1935. They too had no recognizable uniforms until February 1941. Prior to the war, they had enrolled more than one million new recruits. Later they took full responsibility for all groups involved in home defence. First-aid posts came under their control. No one doubted that air-raids would bring casualties of differing categories. Minor injuries could be treated at these posts. More seriously injured people could be treated here before going to hospital. Fortunately, they were not needed as such in Warwick. Mobile first-aid vehicles were fully-equipped.

Evacuees and Refugees

Before the war started, children were evacuated from high-risk areas to the countryside. It seemed a good idea, but not all the

Evacuees in Devon. (Public domain)

potential problems were recognized. Some 4,000,000 mothers, children and others were evacuated and referred to as evacuees (this excluded refugees but included certain types of civil servants).

Allegedly evacuees did not know how to eat properly or use the toilet. Once householders heard these rumours, they were reluctant to accept evacuees into their homes. Being a government directive, it was invoked when cajoling failed. In many cases it was a traumatic affair for all concerned, yet many lifelong friendships were made by others.

Refugees were well-known on the Continent but not in Britain. They had to live somewhere and depended on the goodwill of residents in more peaceful places such as Warwick. After the Battle of Britain ended, it was followed by heavy air-raids on industrial

Battle of Britain poster. (Public domain)

areas and the probability of refugees descending on many parts of the Midlands became a reality. By the 1930s, fire-fighting had become a professional occupation, not a part-time activity.

Some 44,000,000 gas masks were issued. Children under 2 years of age were placed inside a respirator. Masks for under 5-year-olds resembled the Mickey Mouse character. Children soon discovered how to make farting noises with the rubber parts. No gas was used during the war.

Potential Enemies

In September 1939, there were approximately 60,000 German refugees plus other nationalities in England; fewer than 600 of these were considered a risk. Undoubtedly there were enemy agents in Britain, but they were mostly caught, executed or turned to spy for the Allies. Another fear was of fifth columnists. The local Nelson family's German governess was taken away by the police, suspected of being a spy.

The term 'fifth columnist' originated in the Spanish Civil War, when a Nationalist general boasted how he had four armies converging on Madrid with a fifth column of sympathizers ready to support their cause. It was untrue, but spread alarm and confusion. Anti-fifth column propaganda led to poster campaigns discouraging talking in public about the war or where loved ones were fighting. You never knew who might be listening. While there were no reports of fifth columnists in Warwick, these posters would have been seen.

It was against this background that identity cards were introduced. The National Registration Act 1939 became law on 5 September 1939. Registration of all persons living in Great Britain was recorded. Cards should be carried at all times and shown to a police officer if required. Alternatively, they could be presented at a police station within forty-eight hours. Identification of people could be crucial with the anticipated vast numbers of refugees and evacuees moving around the country. The cards assisted with rationing when it came into effect. Lastly, the statistical information would help officials prepare for a post-war country.

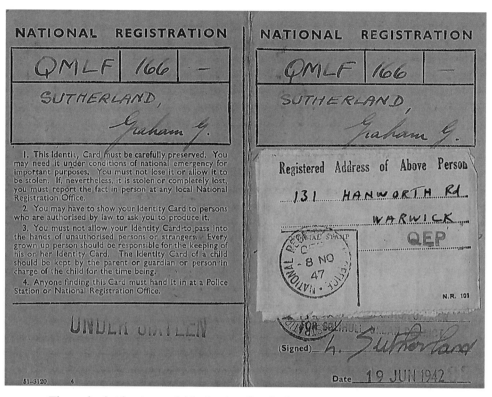

The author's identity card. (Author's collection)

Law and Order

It would be impossible to discuss all the offences committed in Warwick during this period; there was no shortage of them. Those detailed comprise the more notable, unusual or especially relevant to this period, such as bigamy, which was committed by both men and women.

Crime

Traditionally, whenever there were no criminal cases to be heard at court, the magistrates were presented with pairs of white gloves. It happened in Warwick during this period.

The Court Leet is an ancient organization upholding law and order throughout England from the Middle Ages until 1947,

Warwick's Court was founded in 1554 and still operates today. From time to time during this period it commented on matters needing attention.

Magistrates' courts are for the preliminary hearings in the legal system, usually under the control of Justices of the Peace (JPs). They are empowered to deal with initial court appearances or refer them to the Quarter Sessions or Assizes if more serious. These latter two courts have since been replaced by Crown Courts.

Police

Warwickshire was a different county in 1939 than it is today, and included Solihull and Sutton Coldfield with headquarters in Warwick. The chief constable was Commander Edward Richard Busk Kemble, who took command in 1928 following the death of the previous chief. Kemble had no policing background, having been a Royal Naval commander and he kept his naval title. He was a road safety fanatic and ironically lost his only son, Michael, when the rear wheel of his motorcycle collapsed. Kemble was never the same afterwards and his mental health deteriorated.

He was a strict disciplinarian who was generally loathed and feared. Yet he always sent Christmas cards to all his staff on active service. Following the outbreak of war, he moved more or less full-time into the headquarters at the junction of Northgate Street and The Butts. Here he created his own war room where he followed events as they unfolded.

Kemble's deputy was Herbert Scarborough Whitlock Wake, always known as 'He of the Green Ink', this being the colour he used in his fountain pen. If anything, he was worse than Kemble. He was loathed so much that within days of retiring in 1947, his car was totally trashed. The culprits were never discovered, but disgruntled police officers were suspected. It is not an overstatement to say that the Warwickshire Constabulary was an unhappy organization during this period.

Warwickshire Constabulary Headquarters with wartime protection. Note old 'Halt' sign at exit from Cape Road. (Warwickshire Constabulary History Society)

Leisure and Entertainment

There is always a need for leisure time to offset the hours spent at work, and wartime did not preclude this. If anything, more entertainment was provided than before, though much of it was aimed at raising money for needy causes, usually associated with the war. As more troops arrived, they needed something to do in their off-duty time in addition to drinking.

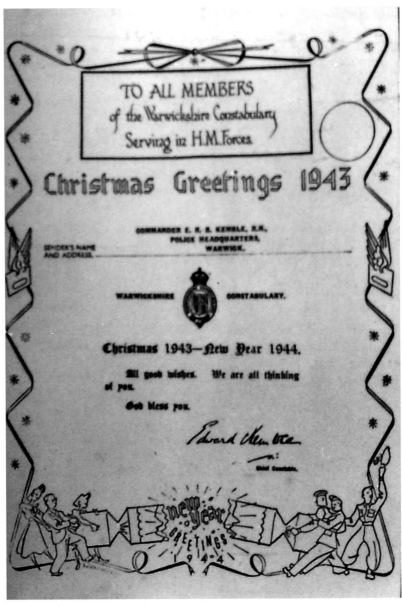

Chief Constable's Christmas card. (Warwickshire Constabulary History Society)

Military

With Warwick being home to both the RWR and the Warwickshire Yeomanry, soldiers were no strangers in the town. Within days of the war starting, there was an increasing appearance of numerous uniforms and tin hats on the town's streets. As the war continued, Warwick became a billet for troops from other regiments, the RAF, American and Canadian forces.

Inevitably there were some conscientious objectors who had to register as such but were not forced into military service. It was not an easy decision to become a 'conchie', as they were called. Regardless of the change of military attitudes, they were universally loathed, abused, lost jobs and in some cases went to prison. Many ended up in non-combatant roles, either from choice or instruction. Women were included and 214 of them went to prison for refusing to do war work. Despite government denials, it is believed that plans had long been in place for limited compulsory military training, also known as national service, which began in late May.

National Service poster. (Public domain)

Rationing and Salvage

War brings hardships, both at the front and back home. Many items taken for granted became scarce. The situation obviously worsened on an island dependent on imported goods. Britain's weakness was realized in the Napoleonic Wars, exploited during the First World War and quickly became German policy in 1939.

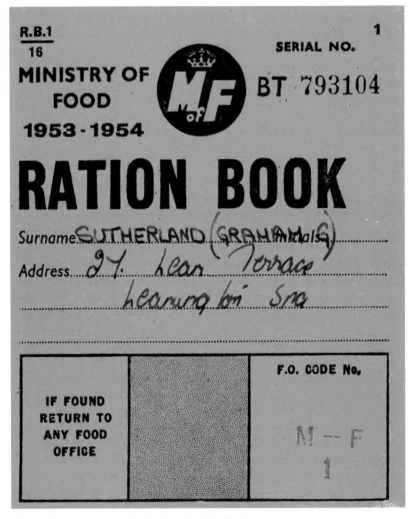

The author's ration book. (Author's collection)

The manufacture of military equipment, closely followed by ensuring that the home population did not starve, were major concerns. Unpopular decisions were made and rationing included many items, not just food and fuel. As luxury goods became scarce, they effectively rationed themselves. Shortages created a flourishing illegal trade known as the 'Black Market' or sometimes just 'the BM'.

Rationing was introduced in stages, beginning on 8 January 1940. If a business transferred to another company, there was no need for people to re-register, only if they moved to another supplier. Ration books and identity cards had to be carried when shopping. Building up a good relationship with a particular shopkeeper might result in being given a little bit extra. Unsurprisingly, ration books and associated coupons were also a prime target for theft. *Agents provocateurs* were widely used and denounced by the media. Rationing of all commodities ended on 4 July 1954, but many youngsters did not understand what this meant as it had always been part of their lives. Alongside rationing was the need to salvage whatever was reusable: today's policies of recycling are not new ones.

Social Issues

Regardless of what was happening elsewhere in the world, social issues arose, some specifically connected with the war. Families were separated for long periods and it is easy to think that sexual needs did not matter. They did. The arrival of numerous evacuees often upset existing boy/girl relationships. Likewise, the arrival of many new men on the scene – particularly American GIs – appealed to many women, creating a raft of problems.

Wars are expensive and have voracious appetites for devouring vast amounts of money. Taxation helped to raise funds but could only provide so much. Extra funding, irrespective of its source, was vital. Without generous donations from people back home, the supply of essential equipment would cease.

Transport

Moving troops and equipment was a logistical nightmare made even more difficult by wartime conditions. Unlike previous wars, disruption from the air was a major problem. At the same time, non-military transport still had to operate. More bicycles were used, causing extra work for the police and courts.

Businesses still had to function, although with a greater emphasis on moving war materials. Tony Atkins remembers

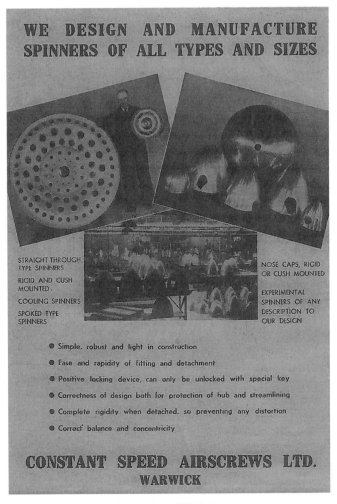

Constant Speed Airscrews advert. (David Unitt)

seeing articulated trailers travelling along the Coventry Road carrying propellers which were nicknamed 'Queen Marys' and seemed to go on forever. They were produced at Constant Speed Airscrews in Warwick.

Many canals were brought back into use. The Grand Union Canal, passing through Warwick, was a busy route for transporting loads of steel, concrete, etc., from London to Birmingham, and returning carrying coal. Many narrow boats were operated by women. Canals also provided a vital commodity for tackling fall-out from air-raids, especially incendiaries: water.

CHAPTER FOUR

Prelude to War: 1 January 1938 to 3 September 1939

In 1938 Hitler announced a union with Austria and German troops were mobilized, followed by Neville Chamberlain's 'Peace in our time' appeasement. During August 1939, Britain and Poland signed a Mutual Assistance Treaty. The British Fleet mobilized, and the first evacuations took place from London. The Nazis invaded Poland and war was declared on Germany.

Children

The school bus service from Wedgnock Park now cost 10s per week, formerly 7s 6d.

King's High School (KHS) fees per term were as follows: tuition, £3 6s 8d to £5 0s 8d; boarding excluding tuition, £21 6s 8d to £23 6s 8d. A dispute broke out between the *Advertiser* and the mayor about KHS's role in the recent gas mask distribution. Neither side backed down. Warwick School (WS) fees per term were tuition, £5 to £6 14s; boarding excluding tuition, £22 to £24. An increase in pupils attending the junior school was reported. WCC gave £4,000 to improve boarding facilities. They obviously knew what was planned because two months later, the same train from Birmingham which brought girls to KHS also brought forty-eight boys who would go to Warwick. They were very thrilled and happy being billeted at the Castle.

Health

1938

When a Coten End School pupil was accidentally blinded in one eye, the school denied negligence and offered no compensation. WCC schools were not insured against accidents. Almost two years later, Mr A.H. Bishop, headmaster of Warwick School had to pay pupil Robert Alex Camkin £750 after he was hit in the eye while on a farm, and a further £64 in costs. He appealed against the verdict and won. The court stated that the 'original case should never have been brought.' Farmers did not want children working on their farms; neither did head teachers want their pupils to help there.

Dennis Unitt, aged 4, of Sanders Street broke up his bed and swallowed a brass knob. He was taken to the Warneford Hospital, Warneford in Leamington, where an operation followed to remove it from his stomach. His parents initially thought it was funny: 'We can easily buy a new one.' One assumes they meant the bed and not the child!

Warneford Hospital, Radford Road, Leamington, 1937. (David Unitt)

Ambulances were very different from today's top-range vehicles. Many were just stretchers on wheels. WBC controlled its ambulance section and their use was not free. Twenty-five calls were answered by WBC ambulances in the four weeks ending on 17 January 1939. Brigadier General and Mrs E.A. Wiggins, Greys Mallory, gave a new motor ambulance to Warwick Hospital. In November, WCC ambulance service acquired fifty-eight new vehicles, but had an unspecified problem with women drivers at night. Less fit volunteers drove hospital cars for transporting patients, sometimes at short notice.

Former Colour Sergeant William Pinfold died in March. Having joined the RWR in 1887, he was captured by the Boers in South Africa. His later postings included India, Ceylon, Egypt and Malta. Another former RWR soldier, Richard Stephen Heath, Linen Street, was found drowned in the Avon. He was awarded the Military Medal and Bar in the First World War and had been a keen footballer. He was in unspecified trouble with the police, and the inquest verdict was 'suicide whilst the balance of his mind was disturbed.'

WBC agreed to construct public conveniences in Cornmarket, Saltisford and Friars Street.

1939

Disease Statistics 1 October to 31 December 1939:

Births: 68 Deaths: 23

Notifiable Diseases:

Cerebro-spinal meningitis: 1 Diphtheria: 1

Erysipelas (acute skin rash): 1 Necrosis (premature cell death): 16

Pneumonia: 3 Scarlet fever: 17

Tuberculosis: 2 Whooping cough: 1

In the approach to war, young men being called up were excused from making hospital payments. Funding for Warwick Dispensary was approved. In April there were only 200 nurses

Nurses' Home, Chapel Street. (David Unitt)

for Warwickshire and another 2,000 were needed. The Warwick Nursing Association had premises in Chapel Street. Although 1,016 auxiliaries enrolled when war was declared, another 3,000 were soon needed. By July, blood transfusion volunteers were tested in Warwick and Leamington.

Red Cross headquarters were at 4 Old Square. WBC let them use the ballroom in the Court House for fund-raising activities, but they had to pay hire charges.

WBC instructed their dustmen to keep lids on bins wherever possible. The state of the tip in the Cape between the Governor's House and the Wedgnock was described as 'an eyesore... smelly...blown about by the wind.' Early completion of the underground toilets in Cornmarket was urged. They were being dug out by hand.

Rear of the Court House and Pageant Gardens. (Author's collection)

Warneford and Warwick hospitals served the area. The Warneford dealt with accidents and emergencies because Warwick lacked the required facilities. This changed soon after war was declared. In May, cyclist Percy Blakeman, Lyttleton Road collided with a motorcycle ridden by Job Collins, Market Street. The collision occurred at the traffic island (still there today) at the junction of Broad Street and Wharf Street, and Percy was treated at the Warneford.

Prior to 1939, Warwick Hospital, including the workhouse, was run by WCC. A Royal Army Medical Corps (RAMC) and a Czech Medical Unit were based there. Nearby Leamington was involved in Operation ANTHROPOID when Czechs parachuted into Prague in 1942 and assassinated SS General Reinhard Heydrich. Their memorial is in the Jephson Gardens, Leamington, together with the memorial to the Lidice residents who were murdered by the Nazis in retaliation.

Today's hospital has changed dramatically. The author's first visit was in 1948/9 and the hospital is almost unrecognizable compared to how it was then. The main corridor remains but

Lidice Memorial, Jephson Gardens, Leamington. (Author's collection)

is now enclosed. Previously it had a roof and was open on the sides, with wards running off it. Supplied with an extra 1,000 beds, along with the Warneford, plans were made to accept overflow patients from Birmingham. The children's wards were decorated for Christmas. The Warneford has long since gone.

Home Defence

1939

ARP

Air-raid precautions in Warwick were organized by WBC and they received £1,000 to set up, equip and pay staff, etc. Wardens considered filling sandbags and digging trenches was not their job. Councillor Harvey was appointed WBC representative on WCC's ARP Executive Committee. Insurance cost 6d per volunteer per annum. Training started at the time of the Munich Crisis.

Following a training exercise, the Borough Secretary complained about the disruption caused to his department, never

Nelson Dale & Co., Emscote Mills. (Author's collection)

mind the disruption that a real raid would cause. He was expected to arrange rescues, decontamination for gas victims, and demolish dangerous buildings, but there was no equipment available and no immediate prospect of getting any. Decontamination vehicles were ultimately provided by local business Nelson Dale & Co.

Eastgate House, owned by Flower & Son brewery at Stratford-upon-Avon became ARP headquarters at an annual rent of £150. It had been suggested WBC purchased the premises and turned them into a cinema. That did not happen and now, instead of receiving some £300 per annum from the building, WBC paid out £150 per annum in rent. The *Advertiser* and other critics made much of WBC's short-sightedness.

Elsewhere the ARP was controlled by chief constables, but not in Warwickshire. Here they became part of WCC, who wanted Chief Constable Kemble to act as their agent but he refused. The wardens were unhappy with WCC and complained to the media.

Eastgate House on far right. The Castle Arms was behind large tree between there and Eastgate Arch. (Author's collection)

Wardens operated a twenty-four-hour telephone service and a siren was situated in The Butts. Factory hooters were banned and only used to supplement sirens. The full test scheduled for late December was cancelled because of torrential rain.

Blackout

A big blackout test took place during the night of 13/14 July between midnight and 4.00 am. It was considered successful by some and decried by others, especially when the wardens were dismissed too early. Rear lights on vehicles were not to exceed 7 watts; oil lamps were banned and acetylene ones not to burn more than ½ cubic foot per hour; hospital cars could use headlights if fitted with a hood and not visible above eye level more than 25ft away: all lights were dimmed by a double thickness of tissue paper. Kerbs were painted black and white. As expected with such unpopular legislation, complaints followed about the blackout being too dark, while the Air Ministry considered it to be poor and needed to be much darker. British Summer Time was extended to 18 October.

Contravening the blackout regulations was an offence. The first offenders, Arthur Frederick Gillingham, the Bear and Bacchus public house, High Street and William Collier, Beauchamp Boarding House, New Street, were each fined £1. More prosecutions followed. One defendant, Mrs Nina Faulkener, Church Street, was fined £1, although she stated a preference for 'going to prison for a rest'. Many motorists ignored regulations, so the police were instructed to rigorously enforce them.

Fire Brigade

The pre-war fire brigade practised monthly. A proposed linking of water supplies with Leamington at Old Warwick Road and Warwick New Road for emergency use needed Home Office approval. The Watch Committee sold the old Dennis fire engine to Courtaulds in Coventry for £200. Seventeen applicants applied to join the Auxiliary Fire Service (AFS), but only those who were medically fit commenced training. Uniforms and equipment were provided by WBC, albeit with a loan from the government. The AFS was formed and trained to fight fires in addition to the professionals. They merged with the National Fire Service (NFS) in 1941.

In mid-January 1939, a cigarette end caused a fire at the Castle Arms on Castle Hill, where the heat cracked many bottles and windows. Special Constables (SCs) complained about not being provided with uniforms when acting as auxiliary firemen, and had to rely on their armbands. Another early-morning fire caused by a fused wireless switch happened in Coten End. The house-owners, Mr and Mrs Clamp, were woken by Jock, their Clumber Spaniel. The Watch Committee declined to send a representative to the British Fire Week at Blackpool. Planned expenditure for the next five years was set at £3,000 but it is uncertain if this included wartime provisions.

Gas Masks

In March 1939 gas masks were distributed to all houses, followed by demonstrations on how to fit those constructed

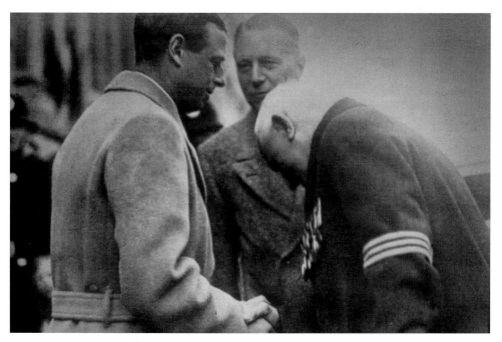

Special Constable wearing armband. Kemble (middle) and Duke of Kent.
(Warwickshire Constabulary History Society)

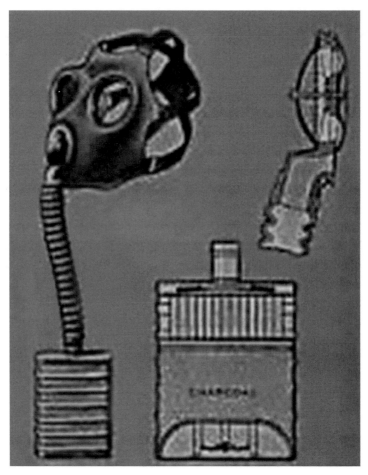

Gas mask. (Author's collection)

for small children. Swindlers charged 2s 6d for checking them. One unintended use for a mask was to pour petrol through its breathing part, which carefully removed any identification dye. With war imminent, people were reminded of how to use their masks, and to carry them always. They were not to be hung up by the head harness, exposed to heat, folded incorrectly, allowed to get wet, and not to be worn until gas warning rattles sounded. Sixteen cavalry regiments still needed masks for their horses. In the Christmas production at Warwick School of *A Midsummer Night's Dream*, Bottom carried a gas mask.

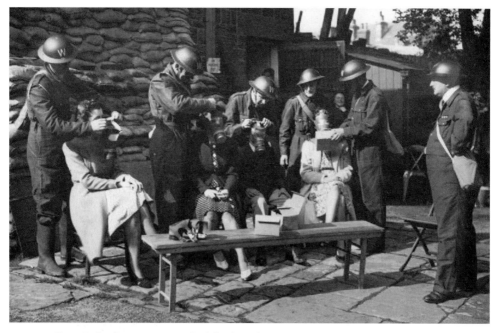

Gas masks demonstration. (Public domain)

Shelters etc

The Earl of Warwick offered to cover the main drive into the castle for use as a shelter for 800 to 1,000 people and offered the use of the castle cellars. WBC accepted his offers, but not the government who decreed that they were 'too far away'. Private basements and cellars were recommended. All Saints Church had already dug out its crypt. The police station was to link up with Shire Hall via an underground shelter. A suggestion to link West Street with Coventry Road by an underground tunnel was impractical.

WBC decided not to dig trenches and to fill in existing ones, with cellars being used instead. It was an unpopular and dangerous decision. In April a permanent trench was dug in St Laurence Avenue, which was rarely cleaned, often flooded and needed waterproofing. WBC provided 84,000 sandbags and shelters were needed for schools.

Limited space in public shelters restricted their use to visitors. Other people were advised to ask householders to

Aerial view of Portobello, a shelter was situated on open land at the junction of Emscote and Greville Roads. (Andy Wing)

share their shelters if necessary. The Portobello shelter, which adjoined the River Avon, held fifty people but regularly flooded to a depth of 18 and was no use. St Laurence Avenue held 225; Pageant Gardens 50; The Butts 50; the Park 100; Priory Park 50; Westgate Arch 50; and Tink-a-Tank 50. By early 1940, this last shelter was not completed following difficulties with the owner of the north wall. The basement kitchen in the Court House was adapted. Extra trenches were instructed to be built at the top of Friars Street to Westgate.

The first evacuees arrived on 1 September and were received at KHS. Here the staff and older pupils filled 300 carriers with 1 tin of corned beef, 1 tin of unsweetened milk and another of sweetened, ¼lb block of milk chocolate; and 1lb of biscuits, carefully counted. These were iron rations to last for the next forty-eight hours.

Law and Order

Crime

With the outbreak of war only days away, confidence tricksters made quick money by fraudulent door-to-door activities selling bargains to help survival in an air-raid, such as fire extinguishers, food, etc.

A mother and son appealed against their earlier conviction for being fraudulent mediums in the Volunteer and Bear and Bacchus public houses the previous year. Their appeals were dismissed, and the original prison sentences of six months remained. The hearing was interrupted when the deputy chairman suffered a nosebleed. Someone put a cold key down his back, but it is not recorded if this treatment was successful.

John Brogdenvitch was sent to prison for eighteen months at the Quarter Sessions for stealing wine, money and other valuables from St Mary Immaculate in July.

The Cavalier in Smith Street, formerly the Volunteer. (John Ashbourne)

The Lord Leycester Hospital with the Bear and Bacchus Inn first building on right-hand side. (Author's collection)

IRA bomb at Milverton Railway Station, 1939. (Warwickshire Constabulary History Society)

In July, an IRA bomb exploded at Milverton Station in Leamington. Although happening outside Warwick, it had a knock-on effect in the county town, and elsewhere.

Police

Garages were to be provided for rural police houses.

Leisure and Entertainment

Pre-war attempts to have twelve-seater motor launches on the Avon instead of self-propelled boats never happened. WBC set the budget for all library purchases at £550. An increase in users was reported, followed by a decrease in book-borrowing immediately following the outbreak of war. This had returned to normal within a month, aided by the growing number of evacuees in town.

Dick Turpin, described as the 'Coloured Warwick Boxer and idol of local crowds', regularly won his fights and became British and Commonwealth middleweight champion. (See further details of the Turpin brothers in later chapters.) Following allegations about the modern army 'being soft', the RWR denied the charge and promoted several boxing contests. Hilary Booth MacAndrew (9) from Cheylesmore, Coventry, was Warwick's first Charity Carnival Child Queen. Passing through many Warwick streets and roads, the carnival finished in Myton Fields. An illuminated boat parade on the Avon completed the day. Glorious weather helped the event to raise more than £500.

ARP county and deputy controllers offered to take off-duty staff home after a Christmas party. Warwickians were reminded how evacuees would need entertaining. St Nicholas Sunday School held a party for eighty children at Wharf Street House. Father Christmas gave them presents, followed by a Punch and Judy show operated by Mr F.W. Allen, superintendent of Myton Hamlet. Public houses remained open for an extra hour until 11.00 pm on Boxing Day.

The Warwick Cinema was opened in March by the Mayoress Mrs Mary Isobel Nelson, usually known as Molly or

St. Nicholas Park
WARWICK

BOATING	:	10 a.m. to 9 p.m.
BOWLS	:	do.
TENNIS	:	do.

Nine Hole Golf Course do.
(Mashie and Putter)

Open-Air Swimming Pool

(Mixed Bathing) 7-30 a.m. to 9 p.m.

SUNDAYS—Bowls, Tennis (grass), 3 p.m. to 6 p.m.
Golf, Tennis (hard), Boats, 10 a.m. to 9 p.m.
Swimming Pool, 7 a.m. to 9-30 a.m. and
2-30 p.m. to 7-30 p.m.

Children's Corner with Amusements and Paddling Pool

Fishing in the River Avon

Cafe and Tea Gardens

TEAS, ICES AND LIGHT REFRESHMENTS.

Car Park

Boat prices at St Nicholas Park. (David Unitt)

CARNIVAL   REQUESTS.

* * * * * * * * * *

Please stand at a reasonable distance from the
    Competitors at Judging time, so that Judges
    and Competitors have the best possible chance to
    do themselves justice.

* * * * * * * * *

Please respect the reasonable demands of the Officials
    and so help yourselves to have a good time by
    helping us.

* * * * * * * * * *

Please pay attention to Loud Speaker Announcements
    as they are made.

* * * * * * * * * *

*Please don't leave Bottles and Crocks about to be broken. They
    are dangerous.*

* * * * * * * * * *

Please do not damage any property on the Park.

* * * * * * * * *

Please make all enquiries at the Secretary's Tent.

* * * * * * * * * *

Please note that Lost Property is dealt with at the Enquiry Tent.

* * * * * * * * * *

Please do not encroach inside the ropes of the enclosures.

Carnival rules. (David Unitt)

The Warwick Cinema, Coten End. (John Ashbourne)

Mol, where Healey Court stands today in Coten End. It closed later in the year for an unrecorded reason and has long since gone. The author remembers visiting there in the post-war years, when one memorable film was *Where No Vultures Fly* (1951). The venue also held a regular Saturday morning cinema club for youngsters.

The County Cinema, St Nicholas Church Street, is also long since gone. The manager was instructed by WBC to confine the queues to the car park and away from the narrow entrance in St Nicholas Church Street. Pedestrians were forced on to the road and into the heavy traffic. If traffic was heavy here in 1938, what would WBC think about today's volumes? During Rat Week 1938, *Your Enemy the Rat* was shown. It was estimated that rats caused annual damage in the region costing £12,000,000 or £600,000,000 at today's values. Suddenly farmers realized that owls were not their enemies as they helped to keep the rodent population down.

Site of the County Cinema, St Nicholas Church Street at St John's, now Castlegate Mews. (John Ashbourne)

A violent thunderstorm in late August 1939 flooded the theatre, the performance was abandoned and it remained closed for a month. As the war progressed, teenagers operated the projectors because there were no adults available.

WBC deemed the Hippodrome Cinema in Edward Street to be unsafe. Its owner, Councillor T.T. Bromwich, said renovation work was in hand and promised more. No further mention of it was made anywhere, so the premises probably closed. They have long since disappeared.

In May Richard T. Holland, secretary of Warwick Cycling Club, married Flora May Varney at St Paul's. On leaving the church, they passed through an arch of bicycle wheels. Dances continued during the war. Even with war looming, the 3rd Annual Portobello Flower Show was held in August, but the October Cattle Show was cancelled.

On the football front, Warwick councillor George Dutton refereed a match at West Ham where supporters of both sides were so unimpressed by his performance that they pelted him with orange peel. Football generally flourished during the war. Horse-racing meetings scheduled for September were cancelled once the war started. Ramblers were advised to 'keep on walking'.

Soldiers' Clubs were needed to entertain off-duty servicemen. One club opened, rent free, in Old Square but still needed curtains, a piano, tables and chairs.

Military

The Auxiliary Territorial Service (ATS) was formed in 1938 as a women's branch of the British army, with origins in the First World War. Employed originally as clerks, cooks, etc., they progressed to more important and heavier duties such as operating searchlights, one of which was situated at the junction of the Saltisford and the Rock.

No. 605 Warwickshire County Royal Air Force Squadron (Auxiliary Fighters) based at Castle Bromwich carried out a mock air fight over Warwick Castle in May.

Social

A fund was started for HMS *Thetis*, a submarine which sank during sea trials on 1 June 1939 with the loss of ninety-nine lives. One crewman came from Leamington.

In 1938, WBC prevented female staff from joining the ATS, citing that their jobs were too important in the event of war. They also agreed to employ a charwoman for twenty hours a week at 9d an hour at the Court House and Pageant House. By 1939, all WBC workers who had been employed for more than a year were entitled to six days' holiday with pay. Two temporary clerks were employed at £3 10s per week to assist with civil defence work.

In June, Roy Vivian Payne from London married Lilian Alice Hedney, Avon Street, the blind organist at St Nicholas, before a large congregation. Her husband was visually impaired, and the couple moved to London.

The Women's Institute (WI) annual conference was concerned about cyclists needing to have rear lights and reflectors. Women's Voluntary Services (WVS) were created nationally in 1938 and were similar to the women serving in the armed forces. Their main function was to assist however they could, such as dealing with general enquiries, keeping information about burials,

Women's Voluntary Services (WVS). (Public domain)

issuing emergency ration cards, etc. They had no itemized job descriptions. 'Services' became 'Service' in 1966.

Transport

Four Warwick residents were injured at Leek Wootton in mid-December 1938. They were passengers in a Midland Red bus which collided with a stationary lorry. Almost a year later, Frederick Chilman, Deerpark Drive was awarded £200 for his injuries and William Collins, Newburgh Crescent £500 for the loss of his wife. They claimed from both the Midland Red company and the lorry driver.

John Wilson, Cliffe Hill, was fined 10s at Bridgnorth for not renewing his driving licence. He maintained that he had forgotten to do so, having lost his original when evacuated from

Banbury/Myton Road roundabout. (Author's collection)

France. The magistrates were unimpressed and considered him 'very neglectful'.

Unilateral parking was now permitted in Jury Street, High Street and Swan Street.

Nationally, it was agreed that the amber light would be kept in traffic lights. WBC budget for pavements in the coming year was set at £1,454. Bad weather in January delayed completion of the roundabout in Myton Road at Banbury Road.

CHAPTER FIVE

Early Days: 1939–40

By 10 September 1939, Britain had been joined by France, Australia, New Zealand and Canada in declaring war and the Battle of the Atlantic began. October saw the first German aircraft shot down over Great Britain. December saw the Battle of the River Plate, off South America.

Rationing began in January 1940. In April Germany invaded Norway and Denmark, closely followed in May by France, Belgium, the Netherlands and Luxembourg. As the month progressed, Winston Churchill became prime minister, the Dutch army surrendered, and the evacuation of Allied troops began from Dunkirk following the German invasion of Flanders. The Dunkirk evacuation ended in June, Norway surrendered and Italy entered the war as a German ally.

The German advances in Europe were generally played down, along with the real risk of Britain being invaded. People in positions of importance were urged not to spread despondency or flee.

In July, the Vichy French Government broke off relations with Britain and the Battle of Britain began. The first air-raids over London in August were followed by the retaliatory bombing of Berlin. As September progressed, the German blitz began in earnest on London and elsewhere. The Battle of Britain ended in October, and Coventry suffered from a very heavy bombing raid in November.

The first few months were known as the 'Phoney War' or the 'Bore War'. However, attitudes changed dramatically with the retreat to Dunkirk and the Battle of Britain. Now the war was treated very seriously with the risk of imminent invasion.

Children

While Warwickshire Education Committee (WEC) agreed that schoolchildren would help with the harvesting as a last resort, the Board of Education refused to sanction it. Schools became workshops. WBC provided schools with stirrup pumps, sand, rope ladders and steel helmets at a cost of £6, which later increased to £8. WEC was asked to contribute to the cost. Fruit-bottling demonstrations were given at the Borough School.

KHS took two parents to court for not paying their fees. Their defence of inadequate shelters at the school was dismissed. They must pay, or their children would be removed. A lecture was given demonstrating recreational physical training. Headmistress Miss Eleanor Doorly was awarded the Carnegie Medal for her children's novel *The Radium Woman*. The school saved £2 10s

King's High School on the right hand side, Smith Street. (Author's collection)

towards an ambulance for Finland. Former Warwick School
pupil, Pilot Officer Peter Cleaver, Emscote Gardens, worked on
salvaging crashed Luftwaffe aircraft.

Westgate old boy Leading Stoker Arthur William Bush,
Crompton Street, had already served for eight years in the Royal
Navy (RN). He fought at the Battle of Narvik and helped to sink
an Italian liner. With Christmas approaching, pupils collected
cigarettes for their old boys who were serving in the armed forces.

Communications

Censorship was a necessary wartime requirement in 1939, but
almost impossible to enforce today. Initially, censorship was
imposed on any reports which might help the enemy, including the
weather. While the press reported names of targets in Germany,
they were forbidden to identify places in England, which had been
attacked. All postal correspondence going abroad was censored.

A new post office opened at 168 Emscote Road with a pillar
box on the pavement – the one in St John's needed a larger
slot – and a stamp vending machine was placed in Smith Street.
Mr F. Hughes retired from the post office in August after forty
years' service and was awarded the Imperial Service Medal. By
November, the Head Post Office closed at 6.30 pm instead of
7.00 pm. An exhibition of postage stamps was held in 1940 at
the museum and the Christmas mail broke all previous records.

On Sunday, 3 September the news of the outbreak of war was
broadcast by radio. A few days later, King George VI broadcast
to the Empire.

Lacking factual knowledge, rumour and disinformation
were rife, as Britain waited in a state of limbo. Before September
was out, the government advised on preventative measures, but
disbelief soon set in when hardly anything had happened, hence
the use of the scornful names above. Everything changed in 1940.
Regulations were regularly ignored if people considered them
unnecessary or else felt 'it doesn't apply to me'. For example,
300,000 people nationally were prosecuted for blackout offences.
This changed dramatically after Dunkirk and the Battle of

Market Hall and Museum. (John Ashbourne)

Britain began. Rumour-mongers were a problem and not necessarily deliberately planted by the enemy. Many newspapers did not have the news on the front pages. These were reserved for adverts, with the news being inside. Reports of the German invasion of Flanders were not immediately visible.

The police moved into the modern era in April and had a new telephone scheme. Private lines connected headquarters to divisions and surrounding authorities. A violent storm in August knocked out forty lines.

Propaganda played a big part in passing information to the masses by any means possible to reassure them. Propaganda derives its name from a seventeenth-century Roman Catholic group charged with Propagation of the Faith. The Ministry of Food urged people to eat more potatoes.

Trains are not a common means of individual communication, but as one passed through Warwick, a porter saw a letter thrown out onto the platform. It was addressed to Mrs J. Clarke, Lakin Road with a note for the finder to post it. The porter ignored this instruction and took it round himself. It was from her brother who was on his way to Warrington Hospital. Unfortunately, she was out, giving birth in Warwick Hospital. Only days later, a mother was in her house overlooking the railway and worrying about her son in Flanders. A train passed by without stopping, but three soldiers were looking out of a window, one of whom was her son. They all shouted 'Mum' and threw out a letter for her. He was safe for the moment.

Food and Drink

Food

Agriculture in Britain was in a serious depression in January 1939. As the year progressed, far-sighted people realized that war was coming and encouraged farmers to grow more food. After September the 'Dig for Victory' campaign began and gardening was promoted. Lawns were replaced with crops, chickens and ducks, etc. Even window boxes were used. Crop rotation was important, along with preserving seeds for the next season. The question of fertilizer and manure was something completely new for most people and in very short supply. Did you use waste food as compost or give it to livestock?

Demonstrations were given on wartime cookery at Westgate School. A man ordered tea and bread and butter in an unnamed local café and then ordered another, but was told it was not permitted. 'What if I came in again?' he demanded. 'Still not permitted.'

By mid-September 1939, it was agreed to pay farmers their subsidies more quickly. Fears of a shortage of farm workers

'Dig for Victory' poster. (Public domain)

greeted the New Year. An appeal for Warwickshire to grow more food accompanied lectures by the Warwick Horticultural Committee. By April there was a serious shortage of farm labourers and the prime minister was urged to release more men from the armed services. Farmers were recommended to utilize grass on roadside verges. Warwickshire roadmen worked on the land for half a day per week between September and November.

Lady Denman commented on how farmers' prejudice dies hard when she had 9,000 Land Girls available for farm work who still awaited employment. The local office operated from 24 Old Square. In February, 110 girls were working on Warwickshire farms. Employing PoWs to work on the land was a controversial topic in the First World War and now became so again. Graham Doughty remembered two PoWs fighting with a bucket. The guards were more concerned about the bucket! Britain was prepared to pay German PoW officers something but had no obligation to pay other ranks.

There was no demand for allotments, so WBC waited for applicants before providing sites. All uncultivated ones were let at half rent. Those in Priory Pools were damaged by dogs. Tractors were available from central pools, but Warwickshire farmers complained about the amount of ploughing they had to do. Five farmers from South Warwickshire were convicted of not ploughing in compliance with government orders. In November, Mr Gunston had not harvested 8 acres of barley to feed his pheasants. He was ordered to harvest it or face prosecution, regardless of how edible the crop would be.

Supplies of fatstock in September 1939 were insufficient for demand. After 15 January, the Ministry of Food became the sole buyer, at fixed public prices, of all fatstock including pigs for slaughter. WCC Livestock Officer, Alfred Anger from Cliffe Hill, was gored and tossed twice by a bull at Coten End Market. His condition was described as favourable. Graham Doughty remembers cattle arriving by train into the Cape Road sidings, then taken to recovery areas in what is now Guy's Cross Park Road. Their thirsty bellows were heard all over the town.

On Wednesdays they were herded down Cliffe Hill into Guy Street to the market at 8.00 am. Housewives complained about the mess and droppings they made on the road and over house doorsteps, etc. They then went down to St John's and to market that way. Casual work was available for drovers who then drank in the Oak, while farmers went to the Crown. Pubs were open all day on market days. Cattle were also kept on the racecourse and slaughtered twice a week. Sheep were also kept there and driven to and from market.

Cape Road railway sidings, circa 1930s. (John Ashbourne)

The Crown Inn, St John's. (Author's collection)

Sheep in West Street, circa 1930s. (Author's collection)

The German invasion of Denmark meant reduced supplies of bacon and pig meat. Mrs Sarah May Payne was fined 10s for not sending her 12-year-old son to school because she needed him to fetch swill for the pigs. She was given seven days to pay but replied: 'I prefer to go to prison.' Children collected acorns for pig food and WBC banned them on housing sites. Humane traps were permitted in rabbit holes. The fine for a first offence for non-compliance was £20; a second was £50.

Chickens were the most popular livestock for home use, with approximately 5,000,000 kept in yards and gardens, providing food, feathers and fertilizer. Rationing ensured their increased popularity. In practice, most flocks were six-strong with an optional cockerel. WBC originally banned them being kept at council houses but quickly changed this policy.

With an impending food shortage in May 1939, exterminating rats became a major priority and a 'Kill a Rat Week' was held.

On the eve of war, the Prevention of Damage by Rats Act was passed, giving powers to local authorities. They remained a problem. Shooting resumed of pigeons and rooks, and sparrows were classed as pests.

The Warwick Branch of the Trade and General Workers Union, J.W. Riley, Peel Road, asked if shop workers' lunch breaks could be staggered to enable them to do their own shopping. It was a national problem, especially where employees worked some distance from home which made shopping difficult and often the best food had all gone before they reached the shops.

Drink

The late September war budget in 1939 immediately imposed increases of 1d per pint of beer and 2s per gallon of wine. A decrease in drink offences was reported in 1940. Ale and beer were never rationed, although their strengths were slightly diluted. Cheap milk at 2d a pint was available for expectant and nursing mothers and children not at school. Families receiving public assistance received free milk.

Following a snowfall in February, an unnamed milkman made his deliveries on skis. Milkman George W. Smith, Hanworth Road, was fined £10 plus £1 11s 6d costs for selling two bottles of milk with false descriptions, which belonged to the Coventry and District Co-Operative Society. It was not his first offence. Plans were made in October to provide milk at midday meals for school children at 4d per meal.

Health

The 1939 annual ambulance competition was won by the St John Ambulance. The police came fifth. Warwick Division nurses struggled to obtain material and uniforms. The Red Cross Headquarters moved to Jury Street at a cost of £1,000, opening in early March after redecoration. Extra funds were raised at an auction in the Market Place. A flag day held for St John

Ambulance and the Red Cross raised £146 6s 7d. A later event for the same causes raised £81.

Within days of the war starting, WCC called for extra beds at Warwick Hospital to cope with the anticipated wounded when they arrived. Wounded personnel added to the demand for nurses, who depended on the vital assistance of volunteers. By 1940, X-ray facilities were available. Efforts were made in December to make it feel as much like Christmas as possible.

Hospitals still had their usual non-military patients. For example, jobbing gardener Walter Reeve (79), High Street, died after falling off a ladder following a seizure in Mill Street.

In August, Derek Anthony Tattersall (17) from Coventry fell into the Avon, opposite Myton Hamlet. Despite rescue attempts by his girlfriend Rhoda Mary Whittley and John Ernest Marchant who worked at the Hamlet, Tattersall drowned. A December inquest returned an open verdict on RWR Private Albert Ernest Moles from Birmingham, who drowned in the canal at Budbrooke. He was engaged to Rose Grabouski from Bordesley Park, Birmingham.

The day before Walter Reeve died, Joseph Hammond, Castle Lane survived after suffering a seizure and falling off his ladder at the Old Bowling Green Hotel. Steeplejack Joseph Whitehead fell 90ft off the Avon Power Station and fractured his spine. Frank Basley escaped unharmed when he fell down a well.

George Walker, Guy Street, was knocked down in Coten End by a WBC vehicle and taken away by ambulance. Three days later, his father received a letter from the town clerk which he thought would be offering sympathies. No, it was a bill for 7s 6d for conveying him to the Warneford and return (6 miles at 1s 3d a mile). WBC refused to back down.

The American Trailer Ambulance Committee donated a trailer to Warwick, which could be attached to any car and had space for two stretchers and four sitting patients. Americans living in Britain wanted to help and show their solidarity with their English hosts.

Bone-setter Matthew Bennett (71), Emscote Lodge, died. He had been setting bones since the nineteenth century and was

Flooded Avon Power Station. (John Ashbourne)

highly regarded and respected. Even while confined to bed, he continued to set bones. His daughter was a masseuse and used electric treatment on her patients.

WBC was responsible for burying civilians killed by enemy action, unless their relatives wanted otherwise. Leonard Toney died at Knowle Villa, Coten End [where the author once lived]. He was a well-known cattle-dealer born in 1878, who rarely left Warwick and lived all his life in Coten End, leaving a widow, two sons and a daughter. His funeral was held at St Nicholas.

A WBC sanitary inspector served notices on properties in Chapel Court, Friars Street, Saltisford and Crompton Street for not using proper council dustbins. Further notices were served on other premises in Saltisford for being in an insanitary state and to comply with earlier notices. They rejected a call for children's toilets, stating that the current ones were all 'scrupulously clean'. The lavatories in the Punchbowl were described as 'not satisfactory' and the owner was 'to put them right'.

Home Defence

ARP

When several French bombers flew over Warwick in the early days of the war, it brought home the reality of the destruction which could be caused by air-raids. WCC's treasures and irreplaceable records needed preserving and many were stored in Welsh slate mines. Believing the Luftwaffe would bomb crop fields with incendiaries, Chief Constable Kemble started Operation MATCHLESS. Police personnel had to watch fields until they were harvested.

The first of several full tests for ARP wardens was held in early January and considered very satisfactory. Local authorities grouped together for mutual aid purposes. Many posts were damp, and more wardens were needed. Along with fire-fighters, wardens had a right of access to buildings to fight fire. While a designated incident officer should be a police officer, a warden might have to stand in until one arrived. Details of all casualties were to be recorded at the sanitary inspector's office in Jury Street. Warnings were issued about not touching any strange objects believed to have been dropped by the Luftwaffe. Following an undisclosed disagreement, the Warwick Division Chief H.J. London and his deputy E.A. Smith resigned.

WBC complained about sirens being used for night-time practice because they disturbed sleep and frightened children! Did they seriously think that the enemy would only attack in daytime? A complaint about sirens being inaudible in the Cape and West End was referred to the chief constable. These were improved, but by 1944 they were considered to be inadequate once again.

Blackout

There were problems contravening the blackout before the Battle of Britain. One night in April, SC Badger found Reginald Watkins Wright in Swan Street who had failed to screen the lights on his vehicle and was parked facing the wrong way. He was fined 5s on each charge, but while being reported had used obscene

A. R. P.

COUNTY OF   WARWICK

NON·BANZ·DROICT

This is to certify that

C

nas been appointed *at Whitnash F.A. Point*
under the Civil Defence Scheme for the County of
Warwick, and this is his authority to carry out the
duties appertaining thereto.

_____
County Controller

Date of appointment ....

Date of issue of card *6·Ⅵ·40·* .... Ref./No. C.S.*18/4592*

Holder's Signature ....

ARP warden's warrant card. (Author's collection)

language and was generally abusive: 'It is a pity they can't find you anything better to do', and added how he also knew the SC's superintendent. He denied this charge in court and the SC had to write down on paper the actual words used and passed it to the magistrates. They found him guilty and he was fined 10s.

In early October, SCs Johnson and Cox reported SC Fred Howell for striking matches out of doors during the blackout. The magistrates dismissed the case, but Howell had to pay 14s costs. He was an SC from Leamington, which still operated its own Borough Police Force independent of the Warwickshire Constabulary.

The blackout was blamed for a road traffic fatality on 16 September when a Nuneaton artillery man was killed on Portobello Bridge. Charles Reading (21), All Saints Road, was fined £2 with 7s 6d costs for obstructing the police at the scene by interrupting and demanding names. Limited street lighting was permitted in 1940, but no beams could be shown. Other refinements followed later. The blackout was also blamed for the increase of cases in the juvenile court.

The Portobello Inn and bridge. (Andy Wing)

In early September fire-watchers on St Mary's tower reported a 'brilliant light' shining from The Butts. It was traced to No. 14, the home of Miss Helen H.M. Madeley, assistant director for higher education in Warwickshire. She was interviewed by Detective Superintendent Alec Spooner and denied knowing anything about it. Then she claimed it was a mistake and blamed her naturalized German housekeeper Vera Hirschfield. In court, Miss Madeley was fined £10 and bound over not to re-offend. Her housekeeper went to prison for one month. She appealed, but the Recorder upheld the conviction and made her pay unspecified costs. Part of the hearing was held *in camera* using photographic evidence from the air. The author believes there was more to this case than was revealed because of wartime restricted reporting, when these punishments are compared with the usual fines for this offence. Also, why was a detective superintendent involved? Was it a signal to the Luftwaffe?

Shop-owners in the winter opened during the blackout, which unsurprisingly caused some complaints. Other shops claimed this was when they did the bulk of their business. The local chairman of the ARPs was fined £2 plus 5s costs at Leamington in November for blackout offences. He had been previously cautioned for this offence.

Evacuee and Refugees

Most applications for non-military billets were genuine, but some were not. False claims were made for the loss of a home and needing money for food. Another scam was claiming billeting allowances for people no longer there. Harold Charles Jones, licensee of the Roebuck, Smith Street, was fined 10s for failing to report the arrival of a Polish alien as the law required.

Mrs Eden, wife of Anthony Eden MP, opened the Young Women's Christian Association (YWCA) hostel in Coten End, serving female members of the ATS and from St John's. Warwick women, whether in uniform or not, could use the facilities. Although generous rates were offered for billets, there remained a shortage. The situation was aggravated by the military authorities also requiring billets.

WEC offered to help with educating evacuee/refugee children. Days after the start of the war, 600 evacuees arrived late at Warwick railway station. The girls were taken to KHS via Priory Park. Education was only one problem; where would they live?

Despite having less than three days to prepare for them, Warwick volunteers rose to the challenge. Somewhat traumatically, the children were lined up like slaves at a market and residents were asked to select which ones they wanted. Pity the children who were left to the end, believing no one wanted them.

Initially Warwick only accepted evacuees from London and Birmingham, provided they did not exceed the available school places. Schools now operated a two-shift system over a nine-hour day. At Coten End, morning school comprised the top two classes and the remainder were in the afternoon. Under 5-year-olds were not admitted and children came to school under their parents' responsibility. A WBC representative attended a meeting in Birmingham to discuss the Government Evacuation Scheme.

The first children arrived soon after the war started. Warwickshire received 6,750 from London. Others from Birmingham and Coventry quickly followed. Warwick and KHS schools became clearing-houses. The Earl of Warwick 'took fifty little guests' into the castle. Allocating accommodation was comparatively easy compared with keeping 5 to 8-year-old evacuees educated and occupied. The sum of 6s a week was suggested as payment to householders, and parents were asked to contribute to this sum. Visiting parents complained that there was nowhere to take their children for food and conversation. Warwick Junior School and KHS helped by opening at weekends.

Mid-June saw the arrival of a further 300 evacuees at Coten End School, where they were fed by the WVS, then moved out to nearby villages. Temporary shelter was available at Marble House. No. 3 The Butts offered accommodation for some mothers and children, having been given blankets by the queen.

Numerous books were donated for evacuees, but there was a lack of billets. The town clerk suggested sending them to Lichfield. For a while, Birmingham evacuees moved to a different area. Southam was full and Leamington was reserved for civil servants. Nos 12-14 Jury Street were available but needed refurbishing at a cost of £255. WBC employed Mr Wheatcroft as a billeting officer at £4 per week. His task was to obtain billets for refugees and he could requisition if necessary.

Other evacuees were moved abroad. Offers of homes came from America, Australia and New Zealand. However, America only accepted better-class children. The government undertook to pay with donations from the parents, except where it was a private arrangement. It was an unpopular scheme and the queen stressed that her daughters, Elizabeth (later Elizabeth II) and Princess Margaret would remain with their parents and stay in London for the duration of the war. The scheme ended following the torpedoing of two ships with the loss of children's lives. Some 170,000 children were evacuated to the USA and British Dominions.

The Reverend A. Hayden from St Nicholas helped escort children going to Australia. Having a wide knowledge of Australia, he helped arrange billets for them, returning later in the year. Canon Keeling took over in his absence.

Following the November raid on Coventry, the Young Men's Christian Association (YMCA) became a refugee centre in Brook Street. The first arrivals were a father with seven children aged from 2 to 14 years. His wife and eldest daughter were in hospital having been hurt when their house collapsed on them. The other children had been under the bed or stairs and escaped injury. They were filthy, and their first request was for water. While their father drank his, the children were given a warm bath and bedded down. More refugees continued arriving and supplies of mattresses quickly ran out. Extra were obtained from WCC and carried to the building by soldiers already billeted there. Volunteer helpers finished at midnight but returned at 7.00 am. The Red Cross and St John Ambulance each donated £50 to the YMCA. More followed.

Lady Willoughby de Broke opened the new canteen in the Congregational church schoolroom. Shortly before Christmas, the Duke of Kent paid an informal visit. A New Year's Eve party was held.

As the blitz intensified, the unofficial practice of 'trekking' began, whereby tens of thousands of people left the cities each night and sought comparative peace in the countryside, regardless of where they slept. Churches, outbuildings, barns and hedges were only some of the places used. Come morning, they returned to their homes and workplaces. The government opposed the practice but, being unable to stop it, they pretended it did not exist.

The author remembers his mother recalling some trekkers she had met. His father had obtained a short pass from the RAF, and arranged to spend it at a country pub. As they were checking in, a family in front of them pleaded with the landlord for a room for the night as all they wanted was an uninterrupted night's sleep. He was unable to help them as all his rooms were taken. After a

The author's father, Iain Guthrie Sutherland (second row down, second from right). (Author's collection)

brief discussion, the author's parents gave them their room and made other arrangements. Sleep deprivation is cruel and even if there were no air-raids in your part of the country, warnings would have been sounded as aircraft droned overhead with bombs and guns crashing. After the Coventry raids, Warwick and surrounding areas gained many hundreds of trekkers and other refugees.

Fire Brigade

A fire in January was caused by a 3-year-old child throwing celluloid onto an open fire in Gerard Street. By May the risk of increased air attacks and possible invasion led to an advertisement for more men or women for telephone duty at the fire station in The Butts. Arthur Robert Bullimore, Greville Road, married Alice Rose Burton, Windmill Road, Leamington. He was a member of the AFS, and they left church under an archway of fire hatchets and onto a fire engine. By the end of the year, the AFS establishment had risen from eight to thirteen and Mr R. Wormell was chief fire officer. Following the lessons learned from the big bombing of Coventry, static water tanks appeared all over Warwick. Another lesson was to ensure that all fire brigades had the same fittings for their equipment. It was no use going to help in another area if the hoses could not be fitted onto their hydrants.

With the Battle of Britain in full swing, fire-watching became very important. Afterwards complacency set in and some watchers sometimes did not turn up for duty. The mayor reminded them that they were committing a serious offence, but the problem continued.

Home Guard

Probably the best-remembered home-based organization was the Home Guard (HG). Often treated as figures of fun, it must be remembered that more than 1,200 of them were killed while on duty. As the war progressed, many people, especially in the areas most at risk of invasion, prepared to shoot at enemy parachutists as they landed. The government insisted it was the military's job and not one for private citizens. Nevertheless, the idea of conscripting often older armed men into a corps was a sound one, the only criteria being that they had to be aged between 17 and 65 and able to move unassisted.

On 14 May, Secretary of State for War Anthony Eden announced the formation of the Local Defence Volunteers, derisively known as 'Look, Duck and Vanish'. Churchill disliked this name and changed it to the HG a few days later. Proper uniforms and weapons were in great demand but short supply. Only minutes after his broadcast, the first five volunteers appeared at Warwick Police Station. Their numbers quickly grew to 200. A large contingent paraded in the Square during August. At the same time, Warwick Aviation Company formed its own HG in Saltisford. They immediately became part of the Crown Forces, held military ranks, carried arms openly, and when in

Home Guard badge. (Author's collection)

Saltisford, circa 1907. (John Ashbourne)

uniform had the same rights as regular forces. Hitler responded by announcing that the Geneva Convention would not apply to them and those who were captured would be shot.

The *Advertiser* instructed: 'In the event of an invasion, no private cars or motor cycles were to be used in the affected areas.' A suggested removal of shop names was not supported by WBC. If the signs included the town, then they would be painted over. The ringing of church bells was banned by the government, only to be rung following an invasion; another unpopular move but appreciated by those who lived near churches. If it was necessary to ring them, only the police or military were permitted to do so. Did they have the necessary knowledge and experience? Once the invasion threat diminished, there was a gradual relaxation of their ban.

Shelters etc

Most school shelters were satisfactory but needed lamps. Where shelters had not been completed, the advice was 'dig in and hang

Westgate shelter, aka The Maze, circa 1950. (Author's collection)

on!'; perhaps not quite the most professional of remarks. WCC
provided £75,000 for Warwickshire schools. Towards the end of
the year, wardens collected warm clothing and toys for children
caught up in raids. A shelter was built behind Northgate House.
Shelters were later provided for householders. The mayor banned

smoking in public shelters and those in the West End and the Cape needed improving. Alderman Tandy was concerned about women and children being denied access to public shelters. The proposed shelter in the Factory Yard was deemed not to be big enough.

The Westgate shelter nicknamed 'The Maze' because of its various projections quickly earned a bad reputation because of all the 'objectionable practices' taking place there. WBC reported that they 'had the matter in hand'. Clearly it was being used for sexual encounters. November was a major problem for the St Laurence Avenue shelter which had flooded. Wardens had been up all night removing more than 100 buckets of water to make it fit for use.

Initially RAF fighters only flew in daylight, leaving anti-aircraft artillery (ack-ack) and searchlight batteries to defend the country. The guns were static or mobile and staffed by men and women. The latter belonged to the ATS and was the closest they got to front-line service.

The problem with ack-ack was what happened to the shells after being fired? Cynics said that more damage was caused by falling shells than by enemy aircraft. During October, Warwick Castle was hit by a stray shell, causing damage to the Clock Tower and other stonework requiring three to four months' work. The cost was not recovered until after 1945. Another shell landed in the Rose Garden but caused no damage. The old castle sandstone fared much better than the comparatively new paving stones. Shells also landed in The Butts.

Coventry

While Warwick suffered only two incidents of enemy action, its resources were stretched to the limit by air-raids in Coventry. Being on the direct route used by the Luftwaffe flying there, Warwick people knew where their target was. Adjoining Leamington suffered more bomb damage and casualties than Warwick, but these paled into insignificance when Coventry was bombed on 14 November 1940, known as the 'Coventry blitz'.

Being an industrial city, sooner or later it would be bombed and indeed it was, several times.

Just before the outbreak of war, an IRA bomb in Coventry killed five civilians and wounded seventy others. By then the city had moved from manufacturing cars to making tanks and other war necessities. It became a magnet, attracting thousands of workers from all over the country, including Warwick.

Following the big raid, which lasted for ten hours, translated from the German code-name of Operation *MONDSCHEINSONATE* as 'Moonlight Sonata', it was mentioned in the *Advertiser* but not until page 4. The front page still consisted of adverts. Once the Coventry and Warwickshire Hospital could not cope, patients were moved out to Warwick, Warneford and Stratford hospitals. One cannot believe the report stating that Warwick knew nothing about the big raid on Coventry. If the London blitz could be seen from Kenilworth Castle, the light from the Coventry fires was so much nearer. Sam Nelson said you could read by its light. Some

Est. 1922 — *Phone 54*

CROSBEE & ATKINS

Building Contractors & Decorators

46, SALTISFORD, WARWICK

Textured Relief Decorations in Plastic Paints

ROBBIALAC STOCKISTS
Wallpapers, etc.

Crosbee & Atkins advertisement. (David Unitt)

6,700 ack-ack shells were fired, but only one enemy aircraft was shot down. Planes returned to France, but it was a short respite as they re-armed and returned.

A reporter from the *Advertiser* visited the next day. He described the city centre 'as a raging inferno…and…organised massed murder', yet he kept a degree of humour. 'The king (George VI) and I made a tour of the bombed areas on Saturday: separately of course.' Other raids occurred, particularly in April 1941 and August 1942, but none was as bad as 14 November 1940. Coventry was unable to fund individual burials because there were no coffins available and 568 were needed. Surrounding towns, other organizations and churches paid for them.

Tony Atkins' family builders business of Crosbee and Atkins covered thousands of miles travelling from Warwick to Coventry carrying out building repairs.

Law and Order

Crime 1940

A gang of thirty to forty unruly children in their early teens regularly ran riot in the Park. They reduced the swimming pool to 'a shambles' and fought mock battles with sticks, stones, bows and arrows and catapults. 'Cannot something be done to stop this sort of thing?' was a popular cry. Something was done and twenty-three of them appeared in court, charged with damage and burglary, which took five hours to be heard. Penalties ranged from fines to being bound over to keep the peace.

Betty Pyatt, Woodhouse Street, assaulted her neighbour, Alice Harris. She told the court that both their husbands were missing, then shook hands with the other woman and the case was dropped. Frederick William Higgins, St Laurence Avenue, assaulted a 13-year-old who he found calling his daughter names and kicking her. Although found guilty, the case was dismissed.

Police Constable Saxby found George Edward Brookes NFA, begging in Albert Street. He had acquired 2s 9½d and was given until noon to leave Warwick.

Agnes Maud Beatrice Perry, Old Park, Wedgnock, was charged with neglecting her five children, one of whom died earlier from pneumonia. Her husband was in France. The house was 'indescribably filthy', and she had not tried to obtain any medical help for the boy. All the beds were covered in layers of carpet and dirty clothes, a jug was covered in dried human filth, and there was enough dirty clothing 'to fill a small cart'. Yet the children had been given some nourishment, mainly rabbits.

Harry Loveridge, Pickard Street, went to prison for one month with hard labour for stealing cultivated mushrooms. He had 'a shocking record'. Franklin's jewellers in Swan Street, opposite Sims of Warwick, had £4 worth of jewellery stolen. Edwin Sims chased the culprits in his car but lost them in New Street.

Armoury Sergeant Christmas J. Williams was jointly charged with Harold J. Titmus with stealing ammunition from Budbrooke barracks. Titmus was found not guilty, but Williams was convicted; he then faced another charge involving Police Constable Samuel Stephen Hardiman, Albert Street. He had been in the police force for nine years and was involved with administering firearms legislation. Hardiman was charged with receiving stolen ammunition valued at 15s 9d. Hardiman had already told Deputy Chief Constable Wake what had happened and unfortunately used the words: 'I have a confession to make.' His solicitor tried to say he had not meant a confession in the true meaning of the word. The magistrates did not accept his version of events and sentenced him to six months in prison. Williams received a similar sentence for both his offences, to run concurrently.

Major Albert Ernest Hayes, (50), Royal Artillery, appeared before Solihull magistrates for bouncing cheques; one was at the Woolpack for £1 11s 6d to a Mr Oliver. He pleaded guilty and asked for a further thirty-four cases to be taken into consideration and received a five-month prison sentence.

Frank Thompson, Hampton Street, Alfred Fletcher and Joseph Harris, both of Peel Road, and Fred Harris, Pickard Street, were charged with trespassing after game with a dog and

The Woolpack. (Author's collection)

a ferret. They maintained they were only on the road. Fletcher had four children and had been out of work for six weeks. He said this case would be 'a wonderful story for Lord Haw-Haw, the Humbug of Hamburg, about the British police stealing the unemployeds' dinner.' The clerk retorted: 'You must not talk politics here.' They were each fined 2s 6d and their nets and caught rabbit were confiscated.

Police

In 1939 Police Constable Arthur 'Pat' Collins lived at 15 Theatre Street and married Margery Beatrice Yardley from Rugby in 1939. A few months after V-J Day, he was woken by a burglary taking place in the Square and went to investigate. The burglars turned on him and soon Pat was fighting for survival. Margery came to help him, but Pat ended up in hospital. Much to the disappointment of the local CID, Chief Constable Kemble called in Scotland Yard. Detective Chief Inspector Robert Fabian took charge and the case was solved. Kemble, in another side of his complex character, held a garden party for the local officers who

Warwickshire Constabulary CID, circa 1935. Alec Spooner (second from left, back row); Herbert Wake (centre, front row). (Warwickshire Constabulary History Society)

had been involved in the case. Kemble's annual salary in 1939 was £800 with yearly increments until it reached £1,100.

The formation of Police War Reserves (PWR) was recommended in April the same year. These were previously retired police officers recalled to duty in times of national crises such as war. Their weekly salary of £3 increased to £3 4s with an extra 6s after the first six months of duty. In the same month the Home Office agreed that voluntary SCs could wear a police uniform. Previously they wore their ordinary clothes complete with a striped armband indicating their position in the police. No doubt the inevitable move to war would have helped to make them more identifiable. The Standing Joint Committee agreed to purchase full uniform for all SCs on traffic duties as follows: four on patrol cars and twenty on motor cycles to include waterproof leggings, etc. and red hurricane lamps complete with posts.

Police garden party: Kemble (*second from right*). (Warwickshire Constabulary History Society)

Earlier, young men were joining the police. A shortage would ultimately occur as policing was not a reserved occupation and the growth of SCs and PWRs would be essential, along with the employment of policewomen. Warwick returned to a full police division in April, under the command of a superintendent as it had been up until 1930. Only days after war was declared, Superintendent Woodward successfully applied to the courts to have several minor motoring summonses withdrawn, stating that he had more important things to worry about.

Douglas Edward Bown and Thomas Oseman, both soldiers, each went to prison for three months with hard labour for stealing Deputy Chief Constable Herbert Wake's car, valued £110, from outside headquarters.

Better protection was applied to police buildings using sandbags mixed with cement. Headquarters had its windows taped up and an armed guard stationed at the main entrance for most of the war. It was not generally known, but one of these armed officers was messing around with his revolver and accidentally shot himself in the foot. Police messengers were to be equipped with armbands.

Five superintendents received a £15 salary increase. All superintendents received a £1 weekly rent allowance.

The idea of employing policewomen had been a thorny issue throughout the country for quite some time. They had been employed by the Metropolitan Police for many years. With police officers being called up for military service, SCs and PWRs went some way towards making up the numbers. Employing women would help make up that shortfall, but the ex-military and naval chief constables totally opposed the idea. Whenever a female prisoner needed searching, one of the men's wives did the job, but it could not continue.

Forced to employ women, Kemble insisted that they were employed full-time with local knowledge and not just brought in to investigate crime. He still fought a rearguard action by making it difficult for women to apply. All applicants were to be single and must resign if they married.

Leisure and Entertainment

H.H. Lacey, High Street newsagent, promoted 'an up-to-date lending library'. During late 1940, town librarian Miss Choat reported that book loans had increased by 4,912 to 26,561 in the quarter ending 30 September. Shops struggled to provide goods for Christmas.

Work resumed in January on the Warwick cinema which was hoping to re-open at Easter, but did not do so until mid-November. Balcony seats were 1s 6d and stalls 8d. Prices included ½d tax. The first film was *The Case of the Frightened Lady*. Laurence Olivier, Merle Oberon and David Niven appeared in *Wuthering Heights*, which was the first film of the year at the County Cinema.

Patriotic music was encouraged wherever and whenever possible. New compositions appeared alongside well-known

```
CALL AND SEE

NORMAN (TEW)
AT THE
PORTO-BELLO
WARWICK

SPACIOUS LAWN          BOATING
On the Banks of the Avon      On a lovely stretch
                                of water.

CATERING               Speciality:
for large or small parties.   COLD SPREADS

        LARGE ROOM TO SEAT 300 PEOPLE

ANSELL'S, "THE BETTER BEER"
```

Portobello price list. (David Unitt)

tunes. A military concert by soldiers was held at the Court House for soldiers. All Saints carollers entertained at the Portobello and other unspecified inns on Christmas Day. A New Year's Eve party was held at the YMCA. Open-air fundraising dances were planned by the Women's Welfare Fund to be held in the Square to provide serving soldiers with comforts. The first parcels were despatched in early March. By May, these dances had raised £37 3s. Dances were cancelled by a government decree following the Nazi invasion of the Low Countries, but Warwick ignored the order and continued as planned, albeit with fewer helpers.

The Castle grounds opened in June for the summer: weekdays 10.00 am to 5.30 pm @ 1s and weekends 2.00 pm to 7.00 pm @ 6s. Prices included a guide. In mid-August Longbridge House opened its gardens from 3.00 pm to 8.00 pm on behalf of the local Nursing Association. There were organized unspecified games planned for the Park. WBC agreed that members of the Pay Corps could use the tennis club for £15 a head to help keep it in good order.

August highlighted the lack of a club for soldiers and their families. Many personnel based at Budbrooke had their weekend leave stopped. They were visited by their families, but had nowhere to offer them rest and refreshments. St Paul's hall was a possibility but needed money spending on it. The mayor donated £10 10s. The existing Warwick Soldiers' Club protested, claiming 'there was no need for another', but this new club opened a month later. More rest facilities were offered for soldiers at the Christian Science War Relief Committee headquarters in Jury Street. Members of the ATS were welcomed.

Military

Army

By 1939 other ranks did not have to carry canes any more. A large recruiting drive and parade took place in Coten End. Fourteen men were successfully attested. Volunteers were joining up, but many more men and nurses were needed. Voluntary service was soon replaced by full conscription, which the Reverend Hayden of St Nicholas fully supported. Young conscripts did not have to pay their hospital contracts.

Following the Munich Crisis, men were encouraged to join the Warwickshire Militia for limited periods of military training. In June 1940 more than 200 men signed up. The first week's training contingent at Budbrooke commented on the food being 'wonderful'. It was working well at the end of August but was quickly absorbed into other military organizations.

Driver B. Wilkins from the New Zealand Driver Corps was the first in Warwick and he stayed with Mr and Mrs H. Miles in Market Street. Corporal Alfred James Williams from the Royal Army Medical Corps (RAMC), Pickard Street, was in Iceland 'where petrol cost 8d a gallon and there was no tax on cars'.

Driver David Frank Osbourne, Royal Army Service Corps (RASC), Hill Street, reported regularly being bombed and strafed in south-east England where he was based.

Former Warwick scoutmaster and Warwick School pupil Lance Bombardier Charles Clayton (32), 131 Hanworth Road [which the author's family moved into during 1947], joined the Royal Artillery battery at Leamington where he instructed gunners. He was awarded the Scouts Gilt Cross for saving a man from drowning. After the outbreak of war, the 113th Light Anti-Aircraft Battery (RA) was formed and moved into temporary headquarters at the drill hall in Coten End.

A Home Defence Battalion of men aged 35 to 50 years was raised in the RWR, which released younger men for active service. In May, Private Angelo Mancini, Emscote Road, was reported as the RWR's first casualty. At his children's request, a mass was said for him at St Mary Immaculate. Major Phillip Woodgate Morley, nephew of John Tibbits, coroner, was killed in action. In July the first service took place in the Regimental Chapel in St Mary's. It would be properly dedicated after the war when members of the RWR could attend. Private Horace William Wiggins, Woodhouse Street, was 'somewhere in Ireland'. So was hairdresser Roland Hodgkinson, Emscote Road, who had refused promotion in order to continue cutting hair.

Warwickshire Yeomanry were reported in mid-November 1939 to be in 'unsatisfactory conditions' at their camp in the Colne Valley, especially with poor rations, sleeping and recreation facilities. The government replied: 'They are not under canvas but in proper buildings.'

Dunkirk

The 'Phoney War' ended abruptly with the invasion of France followed by the retreat to Dunkirk. While the evacuation saved 338,226 Allied troops, many thousands were left behind dead or taken prisoner. One of the author's uncles was successfully evacuated from here with all his men. His mother Lillian Sutherland, was a nurse in Kent and along with colleagues helped

Gravestone at Dunkirk to unknown Warwickshire soldier. (Author's collection)

returning troops during their off-duty time. Seeing the beach today [2018], it is hard to imagine how terrifying it must have been in 1940. France surrendered soon afterwards, making the situation desperate. Government propaganda concentrated on the positive side, but only in later times was it known just how close we were to being defeated. It was some time before stories were published about this battle, and some of them are as follows.

Gunner 'Jack' Baseley (19), Avon Street, had been 'in the thick of it in France', especially at Dunkirk. A former pupil of Coten End School, his father had been a PoW in the First World War. Lance Bombardier George Batty, Wharf Street, lost all his equipment except for his rifle and saxophone which he had carried for 12 miles. Coldstream Guardsman George Pedley, Greville Road and All Saints School, survived when a shell exploded nearby and blew him 6ft in the air. On the road to Dunkirk, he survived on eggs and beer which he found in a farm. Cards were received from Private Frederick Burton, ex-Westgate and All Saints pupil who was captured at Dunkirk. Before the war, he had been a professional roller-skater.

It was whilst on the retreat to Dunkirk when members of the RWR and men from other regiments were taken prisoner by the *Leibstandarte-SS Adolf Hitler* and murdered at Wormhoudt. Despite the efforts of the SS there were some survivors, but the culprits were never brought to trial. The survivors who were later captured by the Wermacht were treated properly as required by Article 23C of the Geneva Convention. The author has visited the site twice and it is a very moving place.

Graham Doughty witnessed a contingent of the RWR arriving back in Warwick with a motley collection of clothes and equipment. They were intercepted, apparently by the regimental sergeant major, who formed them into some semblance of order. His instruction was: 'We marched out and we will march back.' A soldier broke ranks at one stage and went to commiserate with some parents whose son was killed at Dunkirk, and there were tears all round. They received a huge welcome from the crowds.

Royal Air Force

Applications for prospective recruits for flying duties, wireless operating, mechanics etc. were held in 1939 at Shire Hall. There was a higher age limit for non-flying duties. Interviews were later held in Coventry which included the recently formed Women's Auxiliary Air Force (WAAF). The author's father Iain Sutherland (pictured on page 76) enlisted in the RAF, much

Wormhoudt murder site. (Author's collection)

against his own father's wishes, claiming he had more important war manufacturing responsibilities.

Pilot Officer Newell 'Fanny' Orton (24), Bridge End, former pupil of Coten End School, shot down two Messerschmitts over France. Several weeks later he was awarded the DFC. A bar swiftly followed, making him the first pilot in this war to be so treated. A squadron leader, he was killed in 1941 and his body has never been found. Sergeant Observer Ronald Douglas Bailey (26), Woodville Road, was killed in a flying accident, but there are no other details. Acting Squadron Leader Bird, Saltisford, was awarded the DFC.

Royal Navy

HMS *Warwick* was adopted by the Women's Branch of the British Legion helped by the mayoress. Lieutenant G.O. Roberts, nephew of Miss Roberts, High Street, was posted to another ship from HMS *Royal Oak* the day before she was torpedoed. Rear Admiral Sir H.H. Harwood, former captain of HMS *Warwick*, fought at the Battle of the River Plate. With the co-operation of the Admiralty a film was made of the defeat of the *Graf Spee* and capture of German sailors the previous December. Royal Marine Corporal Thomas Henry March, Avon Street, arrived just too late to take part in the battle. Apprentice J.C. Passey, son of the assistant curate at St Mary's, came home after the Battle of the Atlantic.

HMS Warwick. (Public domain)

HMS Royal Oak *memorial at Kirkwall.* (Author's collection)

Rationing and Salvage

Rationing

By early January 1940, Warwick was ready for rationing but some minor adjustments caused a re-issue of permits. For example, 1lb of sugar was reduced to 12oz and butter or margarine was reduced to 4oz, which many considered was insufficient. It was thought better to have these changes ready and not have to implement them later. Quality could not be guaranteed, and housewives must accept what they were given. Same-day delivery could not be guaranteed. Accounts should be paid promptly. Early-afternoon shopping would avoid the 9.30 am to 11.30 am rush period. Carrying home one's shopping rather than having it delivered saved petrol.

The Chamber of Trade recommended all retail shops closed no later than 7.00 pm on Fridays and Saturdays and 6.00 pm on other days. Ration books could be collected from the Court House over a seven-day period and were held in alphabetical order of surnames. Some 16,000 were distributed in late 1939. The Food Controller's office was open from 11.00 am to 1.00 pm and 3.00 pm to 5.00 pm Mondays to Fridays. There were some anomalies: e.g. a permit was required to purchase furniture.

Rationing started in early March 1940 with very few complaints. Butchers and their customers were philosophical about it. Housewives received tips on pickling eggs. The Ministry of Food again suggested that people should eat more potatoes. WCC instructed a special committee at 22 Northgate Street to oversee the shortage of carrots, onions and other vegetables.

Pre-war Foster Bros, Smith Street, sold two-piece sports suits for boys for 12s 6d. Similar suits in flannel cost 8s 6d. Both suits had short trousers. A mackintosh cost £1 1s. These were now rationed. Within a few days of the war starting, coal, electricity and gas were rationed. The government insisted that 'it was to conserve the Nation's fuel, not to cause hardship.' By 1 June, coke was collected from the gas works for £1 17s 2d per ton or £2 2s 2d if delivered. It was only available in 5cwt lots. WBC complained in December about the Miners' Council failing to deliver already reserved supplies of 1,200 tons.

Warwick Gas Works, circa 1940. (John Ashbourne)

Within a fortnight of war starting, food retailers needed to obtain licences from the Court House. Defence regulations made food hoarding an offence. People were permitted to only keep seven days' food in stock. The price of sugar rose by 1d in the £1. Warnings were issued about profiteering becoming illegal.

Books of petrol coupons were obtained from the Post Office or local tax office. Coupons allowed about 200 miles of driving per month. Less vehicle traffic meant more animals using the roads. People who could not afford to run their cars were advised to sell them. Alternatively, their vehicles could be cannibalized to provide useful spares. Petrol soon became a major commodity in the criminal underworld.

Salvage

When waste paper was wanted in late 1939, Warwickshire County Records Office reminded people not to throw out old documents without being examined first. It remained a concern two years later and was raised by Councillor E.G. Tibbits. Ultimately, it was agreed to photograph the existing records. Newspapers and magazines which had been read were used as toilet paper and for lighting fires.

Thames Board Mills Ltd offered to take all of Warwick's waste paper for the next five years. From November 1939 to February 1940 £139,225 was raised from salvaged items in Warwickshire. By March, there was so much waste paper being collected that WBC purchased a hand baling machine for paper, card and clothes for £24. Less paper was now available, and the *Advertiser* quickly sold out. Readers were encouraged to reserve copies. The shortage of paper for newspapers quickly spread. Days later, the *Advertiser* offered to pay 1d for every 3lb of newspapers taken to its office. The idea spread and 4lb of magazines sold for 1d. Between 1 May and 31 July Warwick was paid £132 for collecting 35 tons of paper.

Social

Warwick women met to organize comforts for the troops. Funds were needed for Territorial and Air Force Associations. Businesses asked for prompt payment. The sum of 1d a week saved in conjunction with All Saints raised £66. National Savings made an appeal in Warwick. Since the war Warwick Voluntary Savings for Government had saved £45,383. Their new target was £11,000 a week.

The Heart of England Spitfire Fund Warwick Branch met at the Court House and was given £25 10s by Mr Metcalf from Warwick Aviation Company. This quickly rose to £100. Donations were accepted at Warwick banks and by Mr J. Walshaw, Cape Road. Within the month, Stratford joined the fund which was well on the way to raising £15,000 for three Spitfires. Newell Orton boosted funds when he addressed Leamington and Warwick Rotary Club. Warwick had only made average progress regarding contributing to the war loan. More money was raised during War Weapons Week in which Warwick,

Leamington and Kenilworth aimed to raise £250,000 by giving an RWR concert, talks, films, displays and tanks in the Square, etc. Nearly half was raised on the first day.

The Cinderella Fund was established in Warwick during the nineteenth century for providing 800 to 900 children with serviceable footwear. Children whose fathers were on active service collected 190 pairs of boots from the Court House. Joan Beryl Gardner (19), Leamington, was awarded £35 for injuries received when her arm was caught up in the wringer at the Lord Leycester Hotel. Because she was a minor, £15 went to her grandmother to administer and £20 was invested on her behalf. Income tax rose to 7s 6d in the pound. Local rates rose to 6s 3d in the pound because of the mounting costs of civil defence.

Government loans were available for local authorities to provide alternative accommodation to people while temporary war damage repairs were carried out. WBC was already acting

Lord Leycester Hotel, Jury Street. (Author's collection)

on government warnings about extortionate rents being charged to homeless people.

It was a busy time for the churches. A day of prayer was held throughout Warwickshire a few days into the war. Early in February 1940, the Reverend Delaney Leslie Edmund Saberton, who came to All Saints in 1938, collapsed and was unable to take the service to dedicate a new banner for the Mothers' Union. Later he became engaged to Virginia Dulcie Glover, Thornbank, Leamington. Running the nearby St Edith's hostel was another responsibility until it was sold. During a sermon he attacked rumour-mongers. In December Anthony Waller, Greville Road was appointed Boy Bishop on St Nicholas Day, 6 December, for the third year running. [It was customary in the Middle Ages to choose a boy to act as bishop for the service of the Holy Innocents on 28 December].

The Reverend J.S. Hutchinson left the Northgate Methodist Church after six years and was given a canteen of cutlery as

All Saints Church. (Author's collection)

a leaving present. His successor, the Reverend D.O. Williams, organized a church parade for all troops in the area.

At St Mary's, £2,600 was needed in February 1939 to create a chapel for the RWR. Work started a year later. At the St George's Day service, the civic party all wore red and white roses. May saw an impromptu service in the Beauchamp Chapel which used music shown in the stained-glass windows, before they were removed for safety. The working party provided a quantity of clothes and bedding for wounded soldiers.

The Reverend Hayden at St Nicholas raised £15 8s 11d to purchase tobacco for wounded troops. The Liberal Club received 'thank you' letters for sending cigarettes to the troops. Philip Johnson, Square, raised £100 for cigarettes for the troops.

The sale of the Priory Estate to WCC was cancelled, but later purchased by the Police Authority, notwithstanding the asking price (not quoted) being more than its value. Proposals to erect temporary buildings in the Park were opposed 'unless it was really necessary'. Bricklayers' wages increased by ½d an

St Mary's Church and the Royal Warwickshire Regiment. (John Flaherty)

hour. The treasurer's temporary clerk was paid £2 10s per week. WBC spent £21 1s 4d on a new typewriter.

Government advice was to send pets to the country if possible, complete with items such as leads, muzzles and baskets. If keeping pets, learn where the nearest vet was situated. If being evacuated, they should not be turned into the street or left in a house; better to have them destroyed. They should not be taken to the police but go to a local animal welfare centre. A few days later, the RSPCA denied having destroyed 2,000,000 cats and dogs in the first week of the war. They felt the figure of 200,000 was more accurate. A Warwick woman was committed to the asylum for keeping thirty-five dogs in her house.

According to the *Advertiser*, scouts attended parades and acted as messengers. No doubt those in Coventry had a much busier time. St Nicholas' Group urgently needed somewhere for its headquarters.

The first 120 Canadian soldiers visited Warwick at the invitation of ATS Miss E.M. Brown, who was in Winnipeg when the war started. A great fuss was made of them, although their coaches arrived late. She escorted two men during the day who came from Winnipeg. Each visitor was given a woollen rug embroidered with Warwick's coat of arms, which had been made by disabled servicemen. More Canadians followed. Lord Lieutenant Lord Willoughby de Broke said: 'The Nation is passing through a very trying period. The services of everyone will be wanted.' For the second time in their lives, Herbert Bromage and his wife had to flee from Belgium following German invasions!

The end of March 1939 was 'bitterly cold'. Warwick was hit by violent storms in August with massive floods, cattle killed and structural damage. West Street was a 'veritable river' which flooded the Vine Inn. Luckily the cellars were not affected, and Mr and Miss Wilkinson served customers wearing wellington boots. October witnessed more severe flooding and the Portobello Inn and many nearby houses were flooded up to a depth of 4ft in places. Workers at the Emscote Foundry were sent home. More bad weather followed, and the Warwick School Officers' Training Corps field day was cancelled. February 1940 saw a post-Christmas cold spell with temperatures showing 35° of frost, the lowest recorded since 1893. Many houses were without water. A ban on publishing weather details was imposed, but the *Advertiser* reported the sun appearing for thirty seconds on one day. Many newborn lambs were lost. When the weather improved, people were to be vigilant regarding parachutists. An earth tremor was felt in early July.

Transport

Fewer private motor vehicles on the roads led to an increase in bicycles and public transport. These were quickly followed by a big increase in military vehicles driven by men and women with varying degrees of proficiency. The blackout did not help, and an increase in collisions was inevitable. After being suspended for four months, driving tests were resumed in 1940.

The Great Western Railway was fined £5 for using scales which were inaccurate by 60lb. London Midland Scottish advertised cheap tickets from Warwick (Milverton): e.g. 6.42 am to Blackpool for £1 0s 8d; 9.40 am to Wolverhampton Races for 4s 11d. All fares were singles.

Veteran South African War soldier, Thomas Reynolds (72), Saltisford, was killed by a bicycle in Saltisford during the blackout. Cyclist John Snell from Hatton was not to blame. Warwick cowman Leslie Norman, Thomas Hewitt and Thomas Francis Hobbs, both from Wasperton, drove ten Ayrshire cattle along Myton Road, colliding with a bus. Hobbs was fined £2 and the others 10s for driving cattle at night without lights.

The RAC appealed for drivers to give lifts to service personnel. Councillor George Dutton, Emscote Road, was acquitted of failing to accord precedence to other road users outside the chief constable's office. The magistrates believed his word against the police constable. Parking was allowed in the Square, but the war resulted in a reduction of tips for the attendant. He would now be paid 10s per week to offset the shortfall.

CHAPTER SIX

Britain at Bay: 1941

The British and Australians captured Tobruk, whilst Rommel tried unsuccessfully to retake it. In May, Rudolph Hess flew to Scotland. America froze German and Italian assets in June. Germany attacked Russia later in the month. July saw Japanese assets frozen in America and diplomatic relations suspended. December was a significant month: Pearl Harbor was bombed by the Japanese on the 7th. America and Britain declared war on Japan the next day and on the 11th Hitler declared war on the USA. Within the week, Rommel was in retreat in North Africa.

Children

Borough School Headmaster L.J. Twigger asked dog-walkers to stop their animals damaging the school garden. In July the school provided pupils 'with a well-cooked meal of roast mutton, potatoes, cabbage and a sweet for 4d.' Coten End old boy Sergeant Leadley, Greville Road, was killed in a flying accident [no further details known]. The headmaster wanted 50 to 60 square yards of land for the boys to play cricket. Boxing and golf contests were held at Emscote Lawn at the end of term. Lieutenant Commander Gilbert Lescombe Farnfield RN, DSO, whose family owned the school, was awarded the DSC for his part in the action against the Japanese base at Sabang, Indonesia.

In January, fifty Warwick School pupils spent their afternoons helping on farms. During August twenty to thirty pupils were at

The author as town crier at Warwick School. (Author's collection)

agricultural camp in Berkswell. Town Crier Henry Thistleton made his annual visit to the school in October and awarded the boys and staff an extra half-day's holiday from the mayor. When the author was town crier, he carried out the same custom, but now it is an extra week's holiday; this custom still continues.

Communications

For the first time since the *Warwick and Warwickshire Advertiser* started in 1806, its format changed. News was now promoted to the front page instead of adverts as previously printed. Thomas Turrall, Millers Road, one of Warwick's oldest and best-known postmen, went to prison for eight months for stealing mail. Around 100 extra helpers were needed from

16 to 25 December to assist with delivering the Christmas mail in Warwick and Leamington. The hours were 07.45 am to 5.00 pm with payment details on application. No previous experience was necessary.

Food and Drink

Food

All rough land in the Park was ploughed up for growing potatoes. Subject to military needs, it was agreed that soldiers could be used to assist with the harvest. A surge in demand for allotments occurred when the Dig for Victory campaign started in earnest. Lax holders faced repossession. Market gardener W.H. Cleaver offered to help plough allotments run by women. Edward Langston, Chapel Street, was fined £5 for stealing five onions from a garden. Local boys helped at fruit markets. Strawberries were sold on cabbage leaves specially kept for such purposes because there were no paper bags. Novice poultry-keepers were restricted to a maximum of twelve birds. The WI gave a talk on turning dock and nettles into food.

Spam (an abbreviation of spiced ham) was pre-cooked tinned pork with a long shelf life. Arriving from America, it was not rationed and became a great success.

Drink

Alcohol caused an attempted suicide in Parkes Street. The woman was rescued by her son from gassing herself. Her court case was dismissed, with the police paying the costs. The Queen's Head, Woodhouse Street, Nag's Head, Hampton Street, closed.

Health

The tender of £258 17s 6d to build plus £58 5s 5d to equip a new mortuary, quoted by Crosbee and Atkins, was accepted. It was later described as 'hideous and spoiled the Cemetery Superintendent's flowers.'

Ambulances were instructed to draw their window blinds when treating patients. The Police Authority declined to replace their old hand-pushed ambulances. A big Warwickshire diphtheria prevention immunization programme began. By late 1942, 91 per cent of Warwickshire children had been immunized. The president of the British Legion Relief Organization supplied 10,000 unspecified vitamins for Warwick children. The Princess Royal made a previously unannounced visit to Red Cross headquarters. She was cheered by a hastily-gathered crowd, including some KHS girls standing on the wall at Eastgate House. A place was needed at Warwick Hospital where patients and relatives could gather.

Bombed-out evacuee Mrs Julia Adams (25) was found drowning in the River Leam by a passing stoker and auxiliary fireman. They pulled her out and applied artificial respiration until she recovered and later returned to Mrs E.E. Manley in Wathen Road. Florence Lillian Harridence, Guy Street, drowned herself in the canal by Coventry Road Bridge. She was considered to have been of 'an unsound mind'.

The West End complained that rubbish had not been collected for a month and it was now an intermittent service. WBC approved an application to install toilets in the Warwick Tavern, Crompton Street.

Home Defence

During the year, the organization known as the Civil Defence (CD) Service replaced the existing ARP, AFS, NFS, fire-watchers (now known as fire guards), rescue parties, first-aid posts and stretcher parties. [To keep matters simple, they will still be referred to as the ARP and not by their new title.] Messengers were often teenagers on bicycles.

ARP

Wardens needed another sixty-six stirrup pumps in January. Their chief denied seeking priority in obtaining cigarettes for his wardens. A delivery was expected but he 'did not want the public to think they were going short because of the wardens.' A night lorry driver was wanted at a salary of £3 10s per week. Senior Department Wardens T.A. Bufton and A. Webb resigned for undisclosed reasons.

WBC published details of ARP duties which included recording damage to houses, goods, deaths and injuries; salvaging goods; caring for homeless people and orphans; dealing with lost property; issuing ration books, identity cards and gas masks. If unable to help, wardens directed people to other appropriate places.

More staff were needed, and women were encouraged to apply. Sand was placed around the town for firefighting purposes. A new first-aid post was earmarked for Warwick. A shelter was proposed in Coventry Road between the Garage and the Great Western, an area which was regularly flown over by the Luftwaffe. Legislation now required all commercial premises employing more than a specified number (not given) to provide a shelter for them. The police were to use the shelter on the Priory Estate. By the end of the year, more shelters were planned for the Square and Hampton Street.

On 17 May, James Hiatt (35), 20 Mill Street and Henry Marston (49), 21 Linen Street, were reported as being killed by a fall of earth on St Mary's Common. The media were forbidden to say they had died following a Heinkel dropping bombs on Warwick, possibly aiming for the nearby gasworks. Their bodies were recovered by Police Constable Terry using water divining rods. Henry was an ARP warden who worked for Warwick Aviation. Having served during the First World War with the RWR, he was given a full military funeral. He left a widow and two children. All parties involved were advised to claim for repairs to the culvert, which was damaged and belonged to the Earl of Warwick. More than twelve months later, he had taken no action and was threatened with being reported to the Ministry of Health. Somehow, nothing seemed to happen! During the winter an enemy plane was brought down locally and the HG with the police captured the survivors.

Blackout

Many houses in Cliffe Hill had gates that opened outwards towards the road. WBC advised them about the dangers this caused to other road users during the blackout. May saw Mr Anger of Cliffe Hill in trouble for blackout offences. Soon afterwards, a drunken but well-meaning fire-watcher, Albert E. Easterlow, Wathen Road, saw a light coming from the Warwick Cinema. Going to investigate, he was involved in a scuffle with Police Sergeant Cresswell who had also seen the light. Easterlow appeared in court but escaped being fined. A column of the Home Guard was marching during the blackout in Coten End in late October when they were hit by a motorcyclist. Nobody was badly hurt.

Evacuees and Refugees

The Duchess of Gloucester spoke to some of the Coventry victims in a secret tour of the area. St Mary's was suggested as a possible temporary cathedral to replace the ruined one at Coventry. The offer was spurned, and the bishop stayed in Coventry and did not join the Duchess. In July, Coroner J.H. Tibbits needed a deputy to help with the extra work caused by moving patients from Coventry to Warwick. WBC told him to speak to the Coventry coroner.

A Coventry evacuee was bound over to keep the peace after threatening to kill Mrs Edkins. He had been billeted there, but not any longer. Harry Ernest Rapson of no fixed abode went to prison for six months. He obtained money by falsely claiming that his wife and family had been killed. One of the children taken to New Zealand wrote to say he had 'settled down happily'.

Fire Brigade

Miss Catherine Jarrett (80), St Nicholas Church Street died when her clothes caught light while standing in front of an unguarded gas fire. In June, the town's first steam fire engine, purchased in 1872, was replaced. It provided scrap metal for the war effort. Brigades checked all houses with lofts to ensure that nothing combustible was stored in them. A shed fire in Lakin Road highlighted a problem because there was no water immediately

Coventry Cathedral ruins. (Andrew Walker (*Walker 44*))

available. Firemen had difficulty in finding the hydrant and did not have a standpipe. Everything had recently been reorganized!! It did not bode well in the event of an air-raid on the town. Senior fire officers resigned in protest at the dissolution of the Warwick Fire Brigade and its merger with the National Fire Service (NFS). Later that month, Herbert Morrison, Home Secretary, inspected the NFS at Warwick, Leamington and Coventry. He was treated to an imaginary fire demonstration at St Mary's with four lines of hoses running across Church Street which soon had water spraying over the roof. Taking souvenirs from crashed enemy aircraft was classed as looting.

Home Guard

As the invasion threat lessened, many of the HG became involved with operating road blocks. WBC insisted that its officials could not enlist in the HG and any who were had to resign immediately.

Law and Order

Crime

In November, Thomas Alan Hooson, a NAAFI (Navy, Army and Air Force Institutes) canteen manager bigamously married Miss Doris Mullineaux at Warwick Registry Office. At the Assizes, he received twelve months' imprisonment. The judge commented that 'there were too many bigamy cases in Warwickshire and elsewhere.'

Mrs Margaret Bartlett (48), West Street, went to prison for two months for receiving 2lb of sugar, value 4s, and 6lb of beef, value 6s 6d. Charles and Elsie Kitto, Red Horse, Crompton Street, were jointly charged with receiving 51lb of sugar, 6lb of syrup and 13lb of butter; total value £4 19s 5d. They received prison sentences of three and two months respectively. The Red Horse closed soon afterwards. William James Biddle, Market Place, was fined £100 for receiving a large quantity of building materials stolen from Reading.

Pioneer Private Samuel Todd stole a cap, £2 and a billycan from the YMCA canteen in Brook Street. Going into the Globe, he tried to sell the cap to a customer, who was off-duty Police Constable Hunt. He was fined £1 for each offence. Privates Albert Bloor and John Bill, both of the RWR, stole eight snooker balls from the Rose and Crown valued at £7 7s. Bloor was bound over, but Bill went to prison for one month. Alfred Lewis, Millers Court, went to prison for six months with hard labour for looting bomb-damaged property in Leamington.

Police

Having reserved £257 for constructing dog kennels throughout the county, the SJC deferred this until after the war. The first two policewomen appointments were not posted to Warwick. Anne Briggs Constable who transferred from Leicester was Warwickshire's first policewoman. Their establishment had been set at one sergeant and six policewomen. Sidney Leslie Elswood, Chapel Court, gave PWR Copley a black eye. As Elswood had previously been bound over to keep the peace, he went to prison for three months.

GLOBE HOTEL

(COMMERCIAL AND FAMILY)

Quiet and Homely   Excellent Cuisine

WARWICK

Telephone 144   Prop. JACK HAINES

"Beautifully clean, and most comfortable and delightful beds."

"A comfortable and cosy English home."

"A most delightful place to stay in."

"If Warwick is the heart of England, THE GLOBE is the heart of Warwick."

"As comfortable as home."

"Well worth remembering—comfort and no fuss."

The Globe. (Author's collection)

The Rose & Crown. (John Ashbourne)

The Kemble Affair

No history of the Warwickshire Constabulary during this period is complete without discussing the Kemble Affair. As mentioned elsewhere, he was a controversial, harsh disciplinarian, whose chickens came home to roost in 1941.

The first indications came with a report in the *Advertiser* in mid-August. Two well-known Warwick police officers, Inspector W. Drakeley and Sergeant Joseph Thackman Hall had been demoted to the rank of Police Constable. The *Advertiser* was 'unable to enlarge…but one is suspected to be because of a dereliction of duty and the other very serious. The penalty is harsh with no right of appeal.' Kemble's practice was to punish the offender and his immediate supervisor.

Policewoman Anne Briggs Constable. (Warwickshire Constabulary History Society)

As Sergeant Hall's application to resign was not allowed, he refused to carry out any more police duties. Consequently, he was arrested and charged with 'refusing to obey a lawful order and being absent without leave' under the Defence Regulations. Warwick magistrates described his treatment 'as harsh and tyrannous...incomprehensible to any sane Englishmen.' He had made a false verbal report concerning the loss of some clothing.

Following demotion, he was transferred to Nuneaton, but had refused to go. The facts were made known in court. Despite feeling very sympathetic, the magistrates had to punish him.

Although each offence carried a maximum fine of £10 and/or one month in prison, they fined him 6d on each count.

Kemble was furious and had him re-arrested, re-charged with the same offences and transferred the hearing to Nuneaton. The mayor of Warwick was incensed at Kemble and promptly stood bail for Constable Hall. A fierce denunciation of Kemble followed, led by ex-Sergeant Hall, describing the discipline system as 'based on arrogance, ill-temper and freedom from appeal.'

Warwick's mayor went to court with the chairman of the SJC. The magistrates had no alternative but to find Hall guilty and they fined him 1s on each offence.

Then the SJC asked for a Home Office enquiry into the way the Warwickshire Constabulary was run, suggesting it was on a par with a 'Gestapo State'. The Home Office noted their concerns but refused to change anything in time of war. Hall was dismissed from the force in early October.

Following their enquiry, the Home Office concluded that the Warwickshire Constabulary was not run like a 'Gestapo State'. They accepted that Kemble was unduly severe in some cases, but not vindictive when he felt offenders were prevaricating. Despite its comments, the Home Office declined to offer any redress in the matter. Kemble accepted the criticism and said he 'would be so guided in future'. The enquiry was regarded as a whitewash. The author tried to obtain a copy of it many years ago, but the Home Office and the Public Records Office denied having any record of it.

Also unimpressed was the Association of County Councils who took the matter up with the Home Office. WCC unanimously supported the right of appeal by police officers to their own Police Authorities as had been recommended in 1932, but not agreed by the Home Office. A talk on Police Disciplinary Appeals was given to the Warwick Rotary Club by Alderman T.H. Ryland, 'Democracy is menaced by Whitehall control', and asked why were borough and county police forces treated differently to other organizations and could only appeal to the Home Secretary who was well overburdened with work? The new idea had been rejected by municipal corporations and nothing changed.

Warwickshire Constabulary Headquarters, Leek Wootton, circa 1948. (Author's collection)

The second reading in Parliament of the Police Rights of Appeal legislation occurred in 1943. It made no mention of the Kemble Affair and concentrated on future police amalgamations.

When Kemble's contract came up for renewal in 1948 and coupled with a move of headquarters to Leek Wootton, it was not extended. An upset Kemble returned from London, went home and shot himself. In 2018 the building was put up for sale but months later had been withdrawn from the market and returned to police use.

Leisure and Entertainment

Discarded library books were sent to Budbrooke Barracks. The Christmas appeal by the Warwick Women's Welfare (Parcel) Fund for financial aid for troops in the Middle East was well received. Industrial workers were allowed two days' holiday. St Paul's centre was the venue for a party given by the WVS.

Dances were not always well received, and some residents wanted them stopped. The venues were not identified. Other complaints were made about cars parked on North Rock and the Square when dances were held at Shire Hall. WBC informed the police.

Both cinemas were permitted to operate on Sundays between 4.00 pm and 10.00 pm. These times continued after the war. Propaganda films such as *Target for Tonight* were shown and used for recruiting purposes.

Military

Army

The conscription upper age limit was increased to 51 years. Single women aged 20 to 31 could be conscripted but in non-combatant roles. Approximately 100 to 120 parcels were sent to Warwick troops in April.

Captain Acting Major Frank Thatcher, ex-Warwick schoolboy, was awarded the Military Cross at Bir el Gubi in Libya 'for conspicuous gallantry and devotion to duty'. Communications had been cut, but he ensured that messages got through at great risk to himself. Commando Lieutenant William Frazer was awarded the Military Cross for leading a raid behind enemy lines which destroyed thirty-seven aircraft and a bomb dump. Having escaped, he became a paratrooper. He was the stepson of Major Heath, RWR Depot at Budbrooke. Warwickshire Yeomanry had been twice ambushed in Iran with rescues being made under fire.

Pioneer Corporals John Duffy and Percy Leach stole items from the local army stores. Duffy was fined £2 or fourteen days in prison. Leach went to prison for two months.

Queen's Hussar Phillip Frank Littlewood, Coten End, married Stephanie Mary Bradley, St Laurence Avenue at St Nicholas. He had lost a leg in East Africa. The Royal Tank Regiment thanked Warwick people for their kindness while they had been billited in the area. Many officers revisited the town when they were on leave.

Mrs Beatrice Ellen Nicholls, Stratford, was in the Volunteer, Smith Street, drinking with a soldier, although the pub was out of bounds to him. She tried to hinder his arrest and ended up in court. Described as a widow with three children aged 14, 12 and 9, she insisted that she cared for them but kept strange hours. She denied doing anything wrong but was fined £2 payable within fourteen days or go to prison in lieu. Mrs Eva Emily Mann was charged with a similar offence a few days later, also in the Volunteer. Her case was dismissed.

Merchant Navy

Cadet A.M. Hatton, Birmingham Road, was in a French prison camp near Bordeaux.

Royal Air Force

The mayor described the Air Training Corps (ATC) as 'a nursery for the RAF'. The newly-formed Warwick Squadron established its headquarters in town in April. Squadron Leader B.W. Williams was unable to attend sports day at Warwick School, so he made a flying visit and dived on the school. Spitfire Week in the district raised a total of £15,406, to which Warwick gave £1,884.

Royal Navy

On New Year's Day, Able Seaman Fred Wallington, Avon Street, returned home. He had been torpedoed and spent two hours in the water before being rescued. Initially unable to find his parents, he located them in an air-raid shelter.

The idea of Warship Week was to raise millions of pounds all over the country. Warwick district planned to raise £120,000 needed to purchase a corvette [a small fast naval vessel].

Prisoners of War

Some Warwickians were in Stalag VIII B. To avoid delays with censors, people were advised to write clearly or type if possible when sending letters, keeping them brief as more than one or two per week would overload the censors. 'Stalag' meant a permanent prison camp and was not the name of a place.

Rationing and Salvage

Rationing

Although illegally circumnavigating rationing, the BM was sometimes regarded or excused as bartering for other items and not a crime. The public was urged to report instances to the authorities. There were in the region of 114,000 prosecutions for BM offences during the war. In the immediate post-war years, the author's long-since-dead father obtained a joint of ham on the BM. It hung wrapped in muslin in a quiet spot of the house until his mother found some maggots were in it and threw the whole joint away. Father went ballistic.

People needed to check that they had already applied for new ration books. If not, they must do so immediately. Reducing clothes' rationing to sixty coupons a year had little effect in Warwick, where it was regarded as just another regulation and restriction. Warwick, Rhode Island – its namesake town in the USA – sent clothes and food to the town.

Warwick Borough Food Control Office operated from Monday to Friday from 11.00 am to 1.00 pm and 3.00 pm to 5.00 pm. A points system was introduced, enabling more choice of menus. WCC provided extra cheese and meat pies for its road workers. Charges against the Coventry and District Co-Op for selling bacon and cheese at incorrect weights were dismissed because the inspectors had moved too quickly. In the autumn wild fruit, plums and blackberries were canned and sold.

Salvage

Advertiser readers were asked to become salvage-minded, with fewer newspapers being printed.

Iron railings salvage was a nationwide controversial topic. The cemetery railings had to go. WBC rejected the chief constable's plea to retain those in front of police headquarters as a security measure. Kemble had no friends on the council.

Social

St Edith's hostel housed four people. The Reverend Saberton hoped the new Coventry Cathedral would have 'vision and imagination'. He called Coventry priests 'spare parts' and hoped they could assist parishes housing evacuees. A memorial service was held at All Saints for Montague Reader, Emscote Road, killed by enemy action on the south coast. He had only been in the armed forces for seven weeks. The Unitarian Chapel became a reception area.

Warwick traders blamed the rates increase for retarding their business. Warwickshire roadmen objected to being paid by cheque, which they were legally not bound to accept. However, their expenses could be paid in this way. Emscote Foundry was fined £10 for an injury caused to an employee by a poorly-fenced lathe.

British Summer Time was brought forward by two hours. Grocers closed at 5.00 pm on Mondays and on Saturday afternoons but remained open until 7.00 pm on Fridays to enable women munitions workers to shop. WBC opposed the moves for unspecified reasons, and Thursday became early closing day. Smaller shops were ignored by suppliers of tobacco and sweets, who sold them through their own shops. Queuing caused problems in narrow areas such as Swan Street.

The Reverend C.J. Passey, Stratford Road, needed help in providing necessities for children under German rule in Greece. WBC sanctioned the regular visit of wounded troops. Total rainfall for the year was 21.19 inches.

WCC did not support the proposal to form a regional government. Warwick had now saved approximately £500,000. A warning was issued about women taking care when walking in the Square near the derelict property scheduled to be the WCC new offices. The pavements were very uneven and several women had lost heels or fallen over on them.

The local branch office of the WVS at 12 and 14 Jury Street wanted free use of the ballroom for lectures. WBC provided two writing tables and desks; chairs, typewriter; coal for heating; floor coverings; telephone and waste paper baskets. Beds and some form of light control were needed. They organized a social centre for evacuees and agreed to run the casualty bureau. By early March, 12-14 Jury Street still needed its walls stripping and treating with Walpamur paint. Warwickians lent them furniture with the promise of it being returned after the war. Evacuee ingratitude caused complaints.

A note about Dr Hubert Stephen Tibbits, who married Joan Mary Wharton from Birmingham: the second son of Dr Hubert Tibbits, Jury Street, he was one of Warwick's characters. He survived being knocked down by a car in 1914 and ultimately followed the family tradition of becoming coroner. He heard the inquest into the author's father's death and his kindness will never be forgotten. St Mary's was full for his funeral.

Transport

WBC declined to sanction the erection of bus shelters in the Square. Snow ploughs were fitted to buses as part of WCC winter transport plans. It was estimated that goods stolen on the railways exceeded £1,000,000. Two unnamed Warwick boys appeared at Leamington Juvenile Court for tampering with the railway system, putting it out of order and endangering travellers. They had put pennies on the line at Milverton and interfered with the signalling system. One boy did not attend because he was already in a remand home and the other was put on probation for six months. Putting pennies on the line for trains to run over and increase their size was a popular pastime in the author's younger days.

An increase in horse-drawn vehicles was noticed. In October, Gladys Baxter, Newburgh Crescent, married George Bostock of Weston-under-Wetherley at St Mark's Church in Leamington. She worked in the borough surveyor's office and two WBC horses towed her wedding car. Horace, a gelding, was used by

Market Place. (John Ashbourne)

the Nelson family to pull a barouche or four-wheeled carriage, usually towed by two horses. Horace was unpredictable and might suddenly shy at the old tram lines in Emscote Road or at the rubber strips on the approach to traffic lights.

The Board of Trade released more materials to help recondition prams. Pre-war annual output of new prams was 600,000 which had since dropped to 250,000. Sidney Brewster (75) from Leamington walked out in front of a car in Priory Road, giving Phyllis Annie Freeman (17), Rowington, no chance to stop.

Unspecified complaints were made about the roundabout in Coten End. Other roads were stated to be in a 'disgraceful condition'. Cyclist John W. Randall (28), Charles Street, was killed on the Banbury Road by a lorry driven by Gunner William Campbell Adams. A former Warwick School pupil, John's funeral was held at St Nicholas. The driver was absolved of any blame. Volunteer drivers and vehicles were needed to help employees travel to work as transport problems were affecting manufacturing output.

Warwickians were instructed to immobilize vehicles: 'Some part of the mechanism of the car must be removed in addition to

Warwick Gaol, pre-1934. (John Ashbourne)

locking the doors and removing the ignition key. Secret devices do not count.' Thomas Deans, Rochester Road, Coventry, was fined £10 plus £1 11s 6d costs for being drunk in charge of a motor vehicle. When asked to write down his name, he did so in Latin. 'That is it in Latin: now I will do it in English.' He was disqualified from driving for three months. Eli Pearson was fined £20 for drunken driving but kept his licence. He had demolished Warwick Gaol in 1934.

Anthony Dalzell Hargreaves objected to being told to move his car, which was in the Square, by a label tied to his windscreen. His defence of 'not being able to read' still resulted in being fined 12s 6d for obstruction. When the official parking lots in the Square were full at night, the attendant placed red lamps at the front and rear of cars parked outside these areas.

CHAPTER SEVEN

No Longer Alone: 1942

The first American troops arrived in Britain during January, but Singapore fell in the following month. By mid-April, America was bombing Tokyo, with the Luftwaffe Baedeker raids on English cathedral cities quickly following. In June the Nazis liquidated Lidice in Czechoslovakia as retaliation for Heydrich's assassination. July saw the First Battle of El Alamein and the first American air-raids on Germany. Command of the Eighth Army passed to Bernard Law Montgomery in August, and the Battle of Stalingrad began. On 11 November Montgomery defeated the Germans decisively at El Alamein, effectively stopping German advances in North Africa. It was a great victory and a turning-point in the war.

Children

In January, the House of Commons wanted details of all injuries, fatal or otherwise, involving schoolchildren on farms because schools did not have to provide supervisors. The mayor appealed to the president of the British War Relief Organization for 10,000 unspecified vitamins for Warwick children. Many boys at the Lammas Home for Working Boys spent Christmas with their relatives. Miss Higson addressed the Leamington and Warwick Rotary Club on the moral dangers faced by children in wartime. The mother of a Warwick boy who was determined not to go to school was taken to court by the school attendance officer. The case was adjourned for seven days, during which time his grandmother had taken him to school. (No other details are shown.)

Warwick School was equipped with twenty-four stirrup pumps and forty-eight buckets. Norman Clarke, Westgate School, collected 35lb of rosehips in seven weeks.

The general apathy of Warwick youths caused concern, allegations being made that when they took something on, they soon lost interest in it. This view was very quickly contested. The youth club in Avon Street, which had closed in 1941, now re-opened.

Communications

Several boys and girls from local schools helped with the Christmas post. *Went the Day Well?* was a film about an abortive German invasion of a small English village, something of a forerunner to *The Eagle Has Landed*. People complained about operators taking four minutes to answer when making telephone calls. The exchange replied how the complainers had no idea what was happening behind the scenes with non-stop more important calls taking priority. Telephonists often worked long shifts without complaining.

Food and Drink

Food

More bureaucracy meant farmers must complete forms detailing harvest plans seven days in advance. They were also reminded to surround their ricks with fences which rats could not penetrate. More pigeon shoots were needed. Available land in Warwickshire was increased by 25,000 acres. Prolific letter-writer Amos C. Mills continued writing as he had done during the First World War. He complained about most of the Pigwells still being under the plough.

Warwickshire operated thirty-five camps for volunteer harvesters. Warwick schoolgirls helped at Bourton-on-Dunsmore and camped in the stables at Bourton Hall. They lifted potatoes, washed out pig pens and did general gardening. Younger girls picked fruit at Alcester. An auction in February held for Warship

Week raised £17,000 towards the £120,000 target, which was exceeded by the end of the week. A box of biscuits sold for £110, a bottle of whisky for £150 and a small number of Cox's Orange Pippin apples made £325. Two months later, Walker's Stores in the Square were fined £5 plus 10s costs for selling Grade B potatoes as Grade A at 9d for 7lb instead of 7d per 7lb. The Post Office would not accept packages of blackberries if they leaked. Local children collected rosehips for the government.

L.H. Toney, Canalside Farm, was required to improve the area where he kept fifty cows in a space only large enough for ten of them. Dig for Victory Week was held at Shire Hall with an address by Broadcaster Freddie Grisewood. A.C. Mills suggested that all growing land be nationalized.

In the absence of the real thing, 12,000,000 tins of dried egg went on sale from June. A 5d tin held the equivalent of twelve

Walker's Stores. (John Ashbourne)

eggs costing 1s 9d. A further 24,000,000 tins were kept in reserve. They were off ration and ideal for scrambled eggs and omelettes but should not be confused with egg substitutes. Troops used fire bombs to heat their soup. German rations captured in Libya were found to be inferior. They had lost Vitamin C during the dehydration process.

Alan Page Hunter, Coten End, was granted a decree nisi from his wife Gwyneth on grounds of adultery. She had joined the Land Army and refused to come home, admitting staying with another man in Ireland. Alan was awarded custody of their child.

Drink

Rupert George Robinson, landlord of the Vine in West Street, was fined £52 1s 4d for regularly selling alcohol after closing time. The mayor was unimpressed by some unspecified Warwick public houses and insisting 'improvements were needed'.

A milk sample, source not identified, was described as 'the worst I have ever seen'. The milkman replied: 'It had gone bad in transit.' Milkman James Harold Fletcher, Emscote Dairy, Greville Road, was fined £5 plus £3 'special costs' for selling inferior milk. He had not plunged it regularly in the churns to ensure that the cream was mixed up in it. Milk was of a poor quality in August and had not improved by the following February. Warwickshire was criticized for being one of the counties whose milk yield had fallen seriously since the war started.

People were advised on how best to keep milk in hot weather: 'Keep it in the bottle in a bowl of cold water, which should be kept on the floor in the coolest part of the house. Cover all milk and keep out the air. Use thoroughly scalded jugs and do not mix with other bottles.' The author's grandmother kept milk in this way.

Health

It was difficult to find a hospital bed for a patient seriously ill with tuberculosis. An invasion of crickets, rare in such numbers, interfered with sleep because of their clicking. Tests were arranged in Warwick Hospital for urgently-needed blood donors. In July, soldier Reg Leonard stole 1s from fellow patient Dennis Trevor Wilkins while he was recovering from an anaesthetic. Leonard had several previous convictions and went to prison for four months with hard labour.

Madame Hana Beneš, wife of the president of Czechoslovakia, visited and thanked Warwick Hospital staff for the help they gave to members of the Czech Brigade. On Christmas Day the wards were decorated with coloured paper. Soon afterwards, local children donated 'several small sums of money' from the sale of craft ware. In late August nurses started a 1d a week scheme, aiming to raise £100 per month. The mayor visited, the nurses sang carols, and later provided entertainment in the evening, while there were numerous gifts for the patients.

Barbara Ann Bromwich, Millers Road, died after her nightdress caught light while she sat in front of an unguarded gas fire. Workers from the nearby Park Laundry took her to Warwick Hospital in a van. Charles Doughty from Coventry was found drowned in the canal by the Coventry Road Bridge. He worked in Alcester and was due in court for stealing paper. It was a suicide verdict 'whilst the balance of his mind was disturbed'.

In October the Avon was being polluted by the Baginton Works via the River Sowe. It was still a cause for concern thirteen months later. This had been a regular complaint for most of the first half of the twentieth century. WBC received a complaint about the 'unsightly state' of the toilets in the Cornmarket after servicemen had been to the dental clinic.

Home Defence

During early August, the *Advertiser* reported a young girl being shot in the knee by a German airplane machine gun. The unspecified location was later identified as Warwick.

ARP

The chief ARP warden was given £5 by WBC towards a new filing cabinet costing £10. G.J. Hellon was allowed £23 for using his own car on ARP business. To help with the blackout, the double kerbs under the Emscote Road railway bridge and trees in Priory Pools were painted with white bands. Following the victory at El Alamein, the church bells were rung.

Evacuees and Refugees

A steady return home of evacuees was reported with only about one-third remaining. Sometimes referred to as 'damned strangers', refugees liked the reading room, food and scenery. The new billeting officer was Mr R.E. Page from Leamington. One of the Invasion Committee's tasks was to list any items that could be used by the defenders or destroyed. It was stood down in November 1944.

Some domestic shelters were being used for unspecified 'improper purposes'. School shelters were to be upgraded.

Fire Brigade

A fire-bomb hut, costing £13, housed more than 250 practice incendiaries. The proposed training of 1,500 men and women cost £165, but the hut needed redesigning. WBC ordered all the static water tanks in the town to be sprayed with insecticide. Surface pipes were to be laid between Birmingham Road and the Butts, River Avon to Guy's Cliffe Terrace, Castle Park to West Street and Westgate. Ladders were needed at the Court House and Pageant House roofs for fire buckets and stirrup pumps.

The fire brigade held an information session in the Square concerning air-raid apathy. They asked: 'Do you switch the gas off at night?' Nobody admitted doing so. Their next question: 'Do you like to make a cup of tea during an emergency?' was greeted with laughter. 'Puzzled' asked the *Advertiser* why first-aid workers were driven to the New Cinema for an instructional film and did not walk as the ARP members did. Nobody answered him. A shortage of first-aiders meant they could no longer resource the hospital telephone exchange.

Arthur Thomas Richard Miles, Friars Street was fined £4 plus £1 1s costs for neglecting fire-watching duties in Coventry. Early August entertainment in the Park excluded fire guards who

Warwick gas cooker. (David Unitt)

Warwick Laundry. (Terry Adkins)

were on duty. Watchers at Eastgate House needed one mattress, nine blankets and thirty-two pillow cases. Four watchers received steel helmets costing 5s 6d each, six torches and heard a series of lectures. In June, locals in Avon and Pickard Streets were accused of not helping fire-watchers for Warwick Laundry, who maintained their premises were too big for just three watchers. The laundry supplied more volunteers.

Watchers were trained on a street-by-street basis, hoping to have 1,500 people ready by the autumn, but there was little interest shown. The museum argued that it was not their responsibility, 'but there was a man in Barrack Street.' Eventually the HG took on the task.

Law and Order

Crime

February saw the moustache-shaving assaults. Young Warwick men in reserved occupations seized any man they saw, civilian

Barrack Street, circa 1930. (John Ashbourne)

or military, who had a moustache and shaved it off. Following much criticism of their actions in the *Advertiser*, the practice stopped. It was suggested that they were farm hands.

Florence May Pheasey, Garden Row and Doris Palmer, Chapman Street cross-summoned each other for assault. Pheasey produced a tuft of hair which had been torn out to support her case. The case against her was dismissed, but Palmer was fined 10s and bound over for six months.

Juvenile HG Neville Peabody, Millers Road, finished his night duty and on the way home, burgled houses in Peel Road. He went to Borstal for three years. Days later HG Albert Thomas Hewitt, Humphris Street went to prison for nine months for stealing petrol valued at 12s 6d from Joseph Lloyd of Nuneaton. He also stole boots and pliers and kept a rifle without a licence. An anti-Fenian truncheon was stolen from the Court House. The remaining ones were moved to another wall.

Detective Sergeant Everitt and Detective Constable Russell were in the Millwright Arms when they recognized the coat a customer was wearing as having been stolen from the Globe. They later arrested John Edward Dawes, Lakin Road. Dawes was sentenced to two months imprisonment on each of four theft charges to run consecutively. The officers were commended for their good work.

Leonard Molloy, described as 'an Irish soldier' and previous offender, stole face powder and butter at Warwick railway

The Millwright Arms. (John Ashbourne)

station. He claimed they were for a fellow soldier's wife. The magistrates sent him to prison with hard labour for six months.

George Nelson Dale Co. and R. Hodson & Co. appeared before West Bromwich magistrates charged with giving a false warranty for food containers once containing arsenic in excess of what was claimed. Nelson Dale were fined £5 with £5 costs. Hodson & Co. were fined £2 with £3 17s costs.

Police

The SJC declined to provide medical treatment for officers who were injured or taken ill while off duty.

Leisure and Entertainment

WBC considered that the part of the Avon known as the spillway by the power station was dangerous for boats. In the Park, the

Swimming baths, 1940. (David Unitt)

baths were 'in a poor state'. They were opened a month later in June, so it was assumed that improvements had been made. By the time they closed for the winter, it was described as a 'bumper season'. Admittance was 3d. The prime minister started an appeal for a National Book Recovery Campaign to supply books for service personnel. Headed by the mayor, 4,500 were collected.

Weekly bridge and whist drives had been popular before the war started. Later they became another source of raising money, such as for Warship Week. A Brains Trust was held at the Market Street schoolrooms. There was another large parade in the Square in June involving regular and voluntary groups of all ages, including the ARP etc. and was led by the band of the RWR.

The Pioneer Corps held a concert at the Drill Hall for the bereaved parents of George Gale, aged 4. He had been playing in

Market Street, circa 1940. (John Ashbourne)

Priory Road when a trailer became detached from a lorry, rolled down the hill and killed him. Along with the band of the RWR, they played during the August Bank Holiday in the Park. The idea of holidaying at home was actively pursued nationwide. The Bank Holiday saw numerous attractions laid on in and around the Park, including demonstrations, sports, dancing, music, etc. Complaints inevitably followed, mainly about a shortage of chairs. Nevertheless, it was repeated in 1943. Warwick sent greetings to Louis Napoleon Parker on his 90th birthday. He had produced the famous pageant of 1906, which film can be seen in Warwick's Visitor Centre.

Louis Napoleon Parker. (Author's collection)

Warwickians had a sober Christmas with lower food consumption because of a turkey shortage. On the positive side, church bells were permitted, and St Nicholas recorded a congregation 50 per cent larger than normal. A concert was held on Christmas Eve and Christmas Day in the new Firemen's Club.

An *Advertiser* journalist spent Christmas Day with an unidentified Warwick family. Their son John was in the RAF; another son Robert had been at Dunkirk. Their daughter Kathleen was in the WAAF. Lunch consisted of a chicken which had been raised by the mother and home-grown vegetables. Their thoughts were with the children: John eating a chocolate bar; Robert sharing a comradely atmosphere in an isolated gun emplacement; Kathleen in a shed by a barrage balloon. Father raised his glass in a toast to absent friends which was echoed by his wife 'with tears in her eyes'. After lunch they listened to the king's Christmas broadcast: 'So let us welcome the future in a spirit of brotherhood and make this a world in which, please God, all may dwell in justice and peace.'

Military

Allied PoWs were not allowed all types of books. Those banned included H.G. Wells; anything political and controversial or showing totalitarian regimes in a bad light; Jewish authors; mechanics; George Bernard Shaw or others with a political bias. The parcel fund had raised £76 7s 1d and was now closed because of rationing problems. Christmas was made an exception. The idea was floated of starting a club for wives and mothers of PoWs.

Army

Sergeant Smith, Guy Street, rested in India after escaping from Burma. Landing in Rangoon, he had been ambushed five times, always escaping until his tank was destroyed. He complained how the lack of RAF support left the Japanese Air Force unopposed. Helped by some Gurkhas, he waded through swamps into India. Captain Paul Chadburn (no further details) reported from the desert: 'Life is a mixture of boredom and routine. The soldier's lot is one of dust, flies and unrelenting sun's rays everywhere. No variety of scenery; meals eaten in silence; mental tedium. Only dusk brings relief.' Wireless operator Corporal Pat Doyle, Parkes Street, was recovering from burned hands and face in the Middle East.

A big military exercise took place in and around Warwick with machine guns and a simulated gas attack. The town clerk wrote to the War Office demanding the immediate removal of the stoppage of rights of access on the Common by the Pioneer Corps. However, nothing changed.

Following the rout of the Axis troops in Egypt, an unnamed RWR officer offered each man in his platoon 5s for every 100 prisoners brought in. Major Fenwick, second-in-command, Warwickshire Yeomanry, died of his wounds in Africa. The Yeomanry changed from using horses to tanks.

Royal Air Force

The age limit for ground staff men was extended to 42 years. Sergeant Wireless Operator/Air Gunner E. Merralls, Queen's Square, took part in the raid on Augsburg. Prior to 1939 he worked in his father's blacksmith's business in Castle Lane. He later died of his wounds in 1943, being buried at Cambridge with full military honours.

Royal Navy

Sub Lieutenant Worsley, ex-Warwick School, was awarded the DSC for saving soldiers at St Nazaire, working on slippery decks. Petty Officer 'Charlie' Chaplin, Wathen Road, was awarded the DSM for commanding the 4 x 4in guns on HMS *Penelope* during the siege of Malta. Officers and ratings from HMS *Warwick* visited and gave the mayor a plaque. Parcels of books, toothpaste, soap and socks were sent to HMS *Warwick* with Christmas cards.

A campaign started in late February was accompanied by a procession and other fund-raising activities. Miss A. Griffin, Cape Road won the Warship Week slogan with 'Winston Wants Warwick's Warship'.

Signaller Frank Tandy, Swan Street, son of Alderman Albert Tandy, was serving on a minesweeper and posted to the Malta convoys. Chief Petty Officer Bob Jeffreys, Saltisford, nephew of Albert Tandy, was also serving on Malta convoys and sank a U-boat; he often met up with Frank Tandy. Seaman Charles Bissell, St Laurence Avenue, had been in a tank landing-craft at Dieppe. Seaman Dennis Bateman, Theatre Street, helped evacuate the wounded from Dieppe.

Rationing and Salvage

Rationing

Extra coupons for overalls were available for certain groups of workers in the meat and fish trade. Warwick Gas Company (WGC) appealed for more economy. Allowances for pleasure motoring ended. Only people with a genuine business use had extra coupons. Misuse of petrol became a serious offence.

Salvage

By March Warwick won £50 for salvage collection. Stratford won the first prize of £500 so more was needed to be done. Attempts to salvage bones were hampered by dustmen mixing them in with the general rubbish. The year started with a Waste Paper Salvage Drive. Collecting 1 ton per day could earn Warwick £500. Rubber was much in demand but short in supply after the fall of Malaya. The mayor thanked the town for salvaging 8.5 tons to date, but more was still needed. People with more than one respirator were urged to return their spares to Eastgate House.

Iron railings started being removed in late May. Within days 13 tons of railings, most of them from the cemetery, had been collected but more were demanded. In the following weeks, more than 20 tons of privately-owned railings were collected and others earmarked. The borough engineer heard appeals against their removal; not an enviable task. The gates in front of the Park had to go, but not those in front of the Court House!

Social

The mayor promoted raising aid for China. Funds were needed for a YMCA hut in West Africa. The sum of £340 had been raised by late 1943. Daffodil Flag Day for the Blind raised £74 3s 10d. The *Advertiser* was sold for an undisclosed sum. Thacker and Christmas Ltd insisted on closing at 1.00 pm on Saturdays but opened all day on Thursdays until the end of the war.

A shortage of staff caused problems for WCC, 'who would take steps to defer the calling-up of key employees.' How were they going to do that? Ex-servicemen who were medically discharged had problems finding work. Women who were unable to work in factories were wanted as child-minders for those who could, but were prevented from doing so because of their own children. Interested women were asked to apply at

Thacker and Christmas, circa 1907. (John Ashbourne)

Factory advertisement. (Public domain)

the WVS c/o the ARP at Eastgate House or the WCC Medical Officer of Health.

The first meeting of the Warwick Branch of the Communist Party raised £3 11s. They agreed to work all out for the war effort and 'considered Winston Churchill to be the man for the job'.

The Reverend Hayden, chairman of Warwick Hospitality for Visiting Servicemen, reported receiving more than 2,500 thank-you letters. Described as being 'hidden away' behind the chapel in High Street was Warwick Friends War Relief Hostel run by the Quakers.

Warwick Gas Company wanted to purchase the Common, which begged the question of who owned it? The answer was it had been given to the town and belonged to the people. WBC wanted to acquire it but was warned by A.C. Mills how it could only be done by an Act of Parliament. John Harman Tibbits, chamberlain of the Common, expressed his concern about the contemplated sale by WBC.

Transport

Reginald S. Jeffrey was fined 5s for failing to stop at a 'halt' sign in Church Street, because 'it would have meant getting off my bicycle'. A bicycle was purchased for use by the borough surveyor's staff. Mr J.T. West (87) ran in front of a car in Myton Road and was killed instantly. The driver, Private Vivian Alfred Weston RASC, was only travelling at 30mph and was absolved of any blame. Aircraftsman Thomas E. Payne (21), pleaded guilty to speeding at approximately at 60mph in Myton Road, killing two sheep and failing to stop. He failed to attend court but was fined £5 and disqualified from driving for two months.

CHAPTER EIGHT

The Tide Turns: 1943

German and Italian troops surrendered in North Africa in May. Days later the RAF attacked the Ruhr Dams. In July the Allies landed in Sicily. The Italians surrendered to the Allies and declared war on Germany in October.

Children

Ray Warrington was born on the night of 13/14 June at 3 The Butts. His mother went into labour just as a large air-raid started in the area, undoubtedly aiming for Coventry. Everybody at the home went into the cellar for safety, except for Ray's mother and a nurse. They were moved into the bathroom because the birth was too far advanced.

Miss Gwendoline Rowe, newsagent in Emscote Road, was fined £1 plus £2 costs for employing schoolboys between the hours of 5.30 am and 8.30 am. The boys were unable to produce the necessary permit. WCC arranged to give sex education in secondary schools and was prepared to discuss any problems with parents. KHS geography teacher, Miss Margaret Ethel Watkin, was killed in Leamington when she rode her bicycle in front of a car. The driver was absolved of any blame. She had taught there for thirty years. Mr Bishop, Warwick School headmaster, sat with three coloured USA officers at a Court House lunch. They were teachers back home.

When children reached the age of 17, they had to register at employment exchanges or juvenile employment bureaus, such as

Westgate School. The churches complained about Warwickshire Youth Parades being held on Sundays and clashing with family divine service. In their turn churches were criticized for making youngsters go to church instead of attending other activities. A large parade involving various youth organizations took place, supported by the headmaster of Warwick School, including a service and readings from *A Pilgrim's Progress*. In December, All Saints church was the venue for a rally of youth organizations. The Court Leet made a presentment about soldiers and youths using the children's playground equipment in the Park.

Communications

It was an offence for PoWs to post letters via pillar boxes. They had to use the official arrangements in camp. Patriotic music and poetry were very popular. G. Sykes wrote the following which was published in the *Advertiser* about 'Men of the Fighting Forces having a job to do…eager to meet the foe…to strike, strike, strike…it's the only strike they know.'

Food and Drink

Food

Members of the National Union of Agricultural Workers demanded better wages and hours. Warwickshire members were asked not to strike. By August, there was a great need for women workers in the factories but even more on the land. Help was needed in running hostels for members in Warwickshire.

An ongoing complaint, supported by A.C. Mills, concerned ploughing up the Pigwells for barley again. He wanted to know who paid the rent and to whom. Councillor E.G. Tibbits, currently an officer in HM Forces, replied that the information was not available, but believed the legal formalities had been properly observed, although not shown on any council minutes. The crop was damaged by children and dogs and had been ready for harvesting at the end of August. Three weeks later much of it was damaged by fire caused by sparks from a passing train. Warwickshire celebrated a record harvest.

More pigeon shoots were needed. Rabbits were classed as pests, but also provided an extra source of food and many were kept specifically for that purpose. Killed pest rabbits were a vital source of food or income and were never rationed. The government finally fixed a price for their sale through butchers and effectively stopped many people buying them. Joan R. Harding, Abbotsford, the Square recommended keeping a hedgehog to combat insect problems, especially cockroaches.

Barford farmer Arthur Harold Walter Sparkes brought a cow to market with swollen joints. He was fined £25 plus £5 12s 6d costs and one month in prison, or a second month in lieu of payment. A large crowd attended the Warwickshire Cattle Breeders Association Bull Show and Sale.

Food in restaurants was not rationed but naturally controlled by price and what was available. The new manager of the Tudor House Hotel, West Street was C. Uphill who promoted lunches, dinners, suppers, accommodation, etc. It was agreed, late in the year, to have a British Restaurant but no decisions were made as to time, site or duration. These establishments provided off-ration canteen-style food at affordable prices. Meals cost between 6d and 9d and consisted of soup, a main course and pudding. While the idea grew, a suitable site had to be found. The town clerk unsuccessfully approached WCC for land in the Square by Walker's Stores. Other sites considered were the Pageant Gardens and the Factory Yard.

Drink

Warwick publicans were warned about the number of under-age drinkers in the town. Messrs G.W. Smith and J.H. Potter were refused permission to convert a garage into a dairy. WBC recommended the sale of land near Cape Road at Newburgh Crescent for this purpose. In November Mr E.A. Savage opened his new pasteurized dairy in Guy Street. The Warwickshire Milk Recording Society wound up and donated £110 to the Red Cross and the Royal Agricultural Benevolent Fund.

The Tudor House, circa 1955. (David Unitt)

Health

Elfrida Marjorie, Countess of Warwick's body rested in the Castle for the night prior to her burial at St Mary's. Among the numerous mourners were her mother and younger brother, Anthony Eden. A later memorial service in London was planned. March saw the death of John Tibbits (81), son of Dr John Tibbits. This is an old Warwick family, several of whom have served as coroners. A few days later, the funeral of Arthur Henry Measures of Emscote Road took place at St Nicholas. He had been Master of the Public Assistance Institution for thirty-one years.

The Avon claimed another victim in May. William Henry Moore (16) went bathing in the river with another, thinking it was shallow. Unsuccessful rescue attempts were made by Thomas Hughes, Paradise Street and Roy Henry Davies (16), Avon Street. Roy was later awarded a Certificate from the Royal Humane Society for his efforts. There was a problem at an inquest in October. Henry Peart (43), labourer, had fallen to his death from a window in Smith Street where he lived, but the jury could not agree if he had fallen while drunk or taken his own life. The town crier still opened inquests by calling 'oyez...oyez...oyez'.

Sergeant J.M. Durrant (28) was accidentally shot dead on the rifle range at Budbrooke. All care had been taken. A few days later, Private Alexander Jamieson, a Scottish pioneer, drowned on a River Avon crossing exercise in the Park. Three other men were rescued before it was realized he was missing. An unidentified 8-year-old girl who fell into the Avon in the Park was rescued by Lance Corporal Milton, Monk Street, of the Army Cadet Force, Warwick Company.

The chairman of the management committee of Warwick Hospital protested when he was questioned about the plague of ants on the site, which had now been resolved. He quoted standing orders stating that advance notice was to be given about such questions, which had not happened. Nurses at the hospital were asked to contribute 1s to the Hospital Fund. It was left up to them how they did it. Margaret Teague and Doreen Round, both from Hanworth Road, picked and sold violets to

Smith Street. (Author's collection)

raise funds for the Red Cross. The Japanese insisted that all letters from next-of-kin to PoWs had to be typed. Assistance was offered by the Red Cross and the Far Eastern Prisoners of War Department.

Orders were served on properties in Emscote Road, Lakin Road and Hill Street because of their bad living conditions. The owner of 2 and 4 Hill Street was fined £4 for not complying with them. Various houses [no other details known] were disinfected because occupants suffered from notifiable diseases. Five others were treated for vermin. The sanitary inspector had problems finding someone who would steam-disinfect verminous bedding.

WBC approved the erection of a temporary urinal at the Punchbowl with a public access from Priory Road. It was felt that more discussion was needed over this project. In November, the Court Leet drew attention to the 'unsavoury state' of the public conveniences on Castle Hill, now blocked up, and the Punchbowl and Emscote Road under the railway bridge.

Home Defence

Warwick ack-ack crews gave toys to the children at Warwick Hospital. In conjunction with the NFS, in late November the CD organized a dance in the Court House to raise money for the Red Cross PoW Fund.

Fire Brigade

Prompt action by the NFS extinguished a fire at Rosemount, St Paul's Close. Soon afterwards, Fireman Arthur Short, Linen Street, went to prison for seven months after stealing goods from the NFS Club. Fly-tipping of chairs, shoes, bottles, shrubs, etc. in a static water tank had to be cleaned out by firemen to stop it clogging their pipes. It could have seriously hindered fighting fires. Units from Warwick and Leamington NFS attended a small fire at the Warwick Institute in late October. Despite all the smoke, very little damage was caused. A serious fire happened in Crompton Street in the night at the home of Mr and Mrs Butler. She was lowered to safety by PC Gardner. The interior of the house was severely damaged.

Doris May Stanton (22), Wathen Road, failed to do her fire-watching duty and was fined £1, although the maximum was £100. Watchers were reminded that they had to notify any long-term change of address within twenty-one days. First-aid now amalgamated with rescue parties.

Home Guard

HG Hubert Victor Fulford, St Laurence Avenue, died in mid-January. Six of his fellow HG acted as pall-bearers at his funeral at St Paul's. HG Frederick James Gray, Castle Lane, appeared in court for being absent from duty without reasonable cause. He enrolled in August 1942 and had been warned previously about not coming on duty. When questioned, he said he had been at work at Lockheed in Leamington, which was untrue. It was the first case of its sort to be tried in Warwick and he was fined £5.

Law and Order

Crime

At 7.00 am on 17 May, the body of Mrs Annie Lewis (30) from Leamington, who had died at the Warneford during January, was exhumed in Warwick Cemetery. It followed an anonymous letter to the Pearl Insurance Company saying that she had already experienced six confinements and two miscarriages, and suggested that they made enquiries. An inquest opened at the Court House before Coroner John Harman Tibbits.

Prior to her admission in hospital, she had been treated by Dr Lilian Margaret Fogarty on 16 December, suffering from an 'incomplete abortion'. Annie confessed to attempting a self-abortion using a syringe and water. Her cause of death was shown as 'pelvic cellulitis and septic abortion'. This was later substituted for 'uraemia and miscarriage' and therefore not referred to the coroner, which the first shown cause of death should have been. The certifying doctor, Agnes Leslie, was asked by the registrar to change it. By removing the word 'abortion', she negated any need to refer the matter to the coroner and the police. (Pelvic cellulitis is acute inflammation of the pelvic area. Uraemia is a raised level of urea and other waste products in the blood, normally removed by the kidneys.)

Dr Leslie was unhappy with this instruction and contacted a colleague, Mr Dingley. He agreed with the registrar and stated that telling the coroner would be a breach of confidentiality. Registrar Reginald Wilkins later denied ordering the changes. Matters became more complicated when Home Office Pathologist Professor J.B. Webster disagreed with the first certificate and supported the second one. The coroner agreed that Annie had obviously carried out an abortion, but was unable to prove if her husband knew about it. The jury considered that the registrar had exceeded his duty and the cause of her death was as per the original certificate.

In September, Clifford Lewis, Annie's husband, appeared in court for using his official work petrol allowance for a private matter. He had taken the car twice to his wife's inquest. The magistrate's clerk was John Harman Tibbits who had conducted the inquest, so he offered to stand down. It was agreed that his remaining would not be contentious and so he stayed. His solicitor had asked for the smallest fine possible because of the circumstances. Clifford was fined a total of £10 with 1s costs.

A Warwick girl prepared to marry a soldier, with the church, reception, cake and photographer all booked. Thanks to the photographer, who had been at the first wedding, she discovered that her husband-to-be was already married. Canon Russell advised prospective brides to check with him in confidence about the marital status of their future husbands. No names were shown.

Ernest Meddoms, Coten End, was acquitted of selling sub-standard vinegar. However, his suppliers, London Provincial Vinegar Co. Ltd, London, were fined £30 plus £2 17s costs. Laurence Arthur Malin (18), Greville Road was charged with stealing clothing coupons. Doris Mary Figgs and her sister Frances Ada Hatton, both of Beauchamp Road, pleaded guilty to receiving them. Malin was unemployed after losing a thumb. They were put on probation as this was the first example of such a crime in Warwick, but the magistrates warned people that they would not be so lenient next time. Stealing coupons was a major problem. Arthur William Fletcher (40), The Cape, former chief assistant to the town clerk and deputy executive food officer, went to prison for fraud and further offences were taken into consideration. He blamed the war for causing his physical and mental stress.

Several unnamed people were each fined 7s 6d for not having dog licences. The Earl of Warwick was sued for the £318 outstanding account for the rewiring of his London flat. He maintained that the fees were excessive and offered to pay £21.

The matter was adjourned. A man offered £10 reward for the return of his gold cigarette case to the Punch Bowl.

Police

The chief constable reported that he was 148 officers short and although his establishment was for 7 policewomen, he only had 3. He was relieved of his command for three months to attend training for possible special service in liberated countries to help them re-establish their civilian administration, but he was not selected.

It was difficult encouraging women to join. The standards were high, and few women were able to meet them. Other organizations were recruiting women with less exacting requirements. SC Section Leader Bert Warner had joined in 1920 and retired in early January. At his retirement party at the Castle Hill Restaurant, he was presented with two bottles of whisky (not readily available), and a glass decanter.

Leisure and Entertainment

Two concerts in the Yeomanry Drill Hall raised £1,051 11s 2d for the Red Cross PoW Fund. Since the fund started, Warwick had raised £21,212 4s 3d.

Warwick Darts League held a competition to raise funds for the Wings for Victory campaign. Entry forms were available from J. Sutherland (no relation), West Rock, but for Warwick Teams only. The Dun Cow Fishing Society used the Avon by the sewage disposal works. The possible loss of Warwick Races was announced. A.C. Mills wanted to know who had sanctioned the ploughing-up of the Common to the detriment of sports facilities: 'Expediency was no excuse...sporting facilities should not be harmed.' Mr H.J. Bruton (44) undertook to walk from the New Inn at Norton Lindsey to St Mary's and back in early May. He was allowed a time of one hour, forty-five minutes. It took him fifty-two and a half minutes on the first lap where he was greeted by many well-wishers. Unfortunately, he missed his target by two minutes. He lost a similar wager to Stratford by seven minutes.

Warwick Restaurant, formerly Castle Hill Restaurant. (David Unitt)

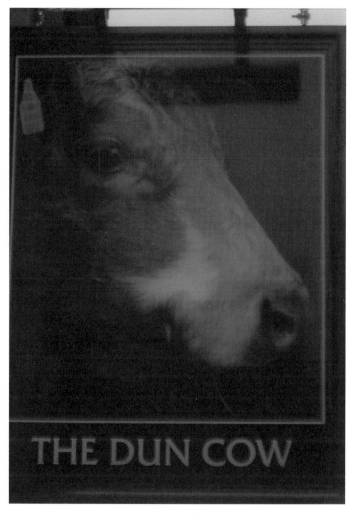

The Dun Cow, Birmingham Road, circa 2001. (Author's collection)

Lord Willoughby de Broke took the salute at a big parade of regular and voluntary organizations. These were followed by demonstrations in the Park of various signalling methods including field telephones, pigeon post and Aldis lamps on St Mary's. Despite calls to 'Dig for Victory', the first-aid post in Lakin Road held a successful flower show.

Military

Americans

Some were brash and vulgar and bragged about anything, but mainly they were friendly and polite. Many Warwick children thought they were 'Men from Mars'. They were generous and the ever-popular 'Got any gum, chum?' usually worked. Often drinking in pairs, they preferred whisky to beer. Troops were regularly entertained at the Court House, usually visiting Stratford, Lord Leycester Hospital, with lunch at Leamington. The Firs, the house where the Nelsons lived, was taken over by Americans for the duration of the war.

No chapter on American servicemen is complete without mentioning 'Kilroy'. He probably started as a piece of graffiti, but no one is sure. The idea grew, and his name appeared in various and often unusual places. Both Hitler and Stalin thought he was a spy. Regardless of how hard one looked, he was never found because…'Kilroy was here'…but long since gone. He was the American version of Chad of 'Wot no…' fame with his face peering over a wall.

Army

All males born between 1 July and 30 September 1925 now had to register for conscription.

Aubrey Victor Langston, Chapel Street, was wounded in the leg fighting in the desert. He was described thus by his commanding officer: 'I would like you to know how well he has done: he has played his part in many successful battles.' Sergeant T.G. Pantry, Aylesford Temperance Hotel, High Street, married Miss Rita Azzopardi in Malta, where her father was an important man. W. Gilks, nephew of Mr and Mrs W. Hall, Station Avenue, 'where he made his home', was awarded the Military Medal. On leaving school he had joined the King's Hussars, spending six years on the North-West Frontier of India. Leaving the army in 1938, he was employed by Warwick Aviation but later recalled to the Staffordshire Yeomanry and was currently in the Middle East.

Merchant Navy

A Comforts Fund was started.

Royal Air Force

Big air attacks were mounted on France and Belgium. A unit of Kittyhawk bombers, commanded by Group Captain John Darwen DFC from Warwick, sank twenty-three Axis ships in the Straits of Messina evacuating German troops from Sicily. Squadron Leader Geoffrey Cockayne Hyde, Cliffe Hill was killed on the Dieppe Raid. He was buried nearby at Hautot.

Another 'Wings for Victory Week' scheme was started which asked housewives to donate aluminium pots, etc. The figure of £307,439 was raised in the Warwick District, which had hoped to raise £200,000.

Royal Navy

Fleet Air Arm Observer Sub Lieutenant W.N. Jones (21), Rosedene, Paradise Street, completed his second tour of duty on Malta, where he flew in fifty strikes against the enemy and logged 540 hours' flying time, which was a record. His plane sank eight enemy ships.

Prisoners of War

Italians working on the land were accommodated in a camp on the Common or special billets on farms, but always under the control of the camp commandant. They roamed free for up to 1 mile from their billets when not on duty. Fraternizing with PoWs was considered unpatriotic, especially for females, but it still happened.

Rationing and Salvage

Rationing

Fines from £5 to £30 were issued by Warwick magistrates for petrol misuse.

Salvage

Anything made of metal was wanted, including hairpins and combs which quickly disappeared from the shops. Room 69 at Warwick Castle became the temporary headquarters for the local district scrap metal drive. Here a team of three women sorted the scrap. Reminders were issued not to throw away rubber rings from bottle-stoppers.

Re-using and adapting other items became the norm. Some of the following make-do measures were used in Warwick. If no hinges were available, other materials such as leather were used. Kellogg's cornflake packets helped repair shoes and were always claimed by the person who had the last portion. Flour sacks from Kench's Mill made nightdresses and pigs' bladders made temporary footballs. Nails were removed carefully, straightened and re-used. In the run-up to Christmas, the WVS held a make-do-and-mend session in Jury Street, showing how to renovate items and demonstrating wartime recipes.

Kench's Mill, 1908. (John Ashbourne)

Social

All Saints Church was reported as being free from debt. At St Mary's, Canon C.A.H. Russell suffered from a strained heart and was instructed to walk more slowly. Battle of Britain Sunday was celebrated in conjunction with Harvest Festival. There were no spare seats for the Remembrance Day Service and vast crowds stood at the war memorial. Later that month the Judges Legal Service was held, as it still is today, despite the law courts having moved to Leamington. This service marks the beginning of the legal year.

During the fortnight from 17 June, billets were found for 24 nurses; 40 females for Lockheed in Leamington; 20 transferred labour; 6 from the Admiralty; 8 evacuees from other towns; and 26 others.

Miss Freda Blakewater, Parkes Street, raised 17s 6d for the Aid to Russia Fund by raffling her Snow White and the Seven Dwarfs figures. She received a letter of thanks from Mrs Churchill at 10 Downing Street. The mayoress led a group of women making comforts for the women and children of Russia. Wool cost 2s 6d a pound and she needed more money. Women were needed to work preparing synthetic jewels for electronic aircraft instruments in 'an old Warwickshire garden'. This venue was not disclosed.

The first suggestions for developing post-war Warwick appeared in a booklet. All new houses nationwide were to include space for a pram and a pushbike. A.C. Mills agreed with Alderman Holmes about the number of houses in Warwick which should be demolished.

WBC presented a bill in Parliament to acquire ownership of the Common including the racecourse but it was postponed for a year. WBC was prepared to support the sale of the Common to the Gas Company. Councillor E.G. Tibbits was concerned about the lack of WBC opposition to these expansion plans.

Judge A.R. Kennedy sitting in the County Court was appalled at the state of a house in Emscote Road. The landlord had taken the occupant, Mrs Mancini, to court for repossession after rent arrears of £5 2s 6d. A widow with several children, she existed on a war pension of £1 1s per week and 7s 6d from a lodger. She paid her rent on condition that the landlord repaired the house; he had not done so, therefore his rent was withheld. Judge Kennedy adjourned the case, but then he died a week later. The final outcome was not shown.

A proposed amalgamation of Warwick with Leamington was rejected by WBC by thirteen votes to six. It was agreed to pay the mayor £150 per annum towards his expenses.

The 6th Warwick Wolf Cubs camped at Hampton-on-the-Hill. The Court Leet asked for the brook in the Park to be cleared of rubbish to prevent flooding near the putting green.

Transport

Two Leamington men were fined £1 for cycling in the Park. Cyclists regularly ignored the traffic signs and rode up Smith Street.

WBC received complaints about the Midland Red not stopping at intermediate stops on the late-night service from Leamington to Warwick; not accepting intermediate bus fares; and buses from Stratford not stopping at St Laurence Avenue, despite being requested to do so.

Patrick Joseph Lawton (43), Upper Cape, walked to Leamington railway station in the road to meet his sailor son home on leave. He had been drinking and was run down by a car. The driver was not to blame. Patrick left a widow, two daughters and four sons. He had fought in the Royal Irish Regiment during the First World War and later in the Army of Occupation until 1921. His eldest son was a gunner in the RAF in the Middle East.

Just before Christmas, William Frederick Elliman (42), Greville Road, was cycling down Smith Street when he was killed by a military lorry from Birmingham, which did not stop. William was sober and there were lights on his bicycle. He left a widow and five children. The lorry-driver was Albert Edward Andrews who said he felt a bump and thought he had hit the kerb. A verdict of accidental death was recorded.

Damage caused by horses in the cemetery cost £14 6s 9d.

CHAPTER NINE

On the Attack: 1944

On 6 June the D-Day landings took place in France, followed a week later by the first German V-1 rockets being launched at Britain. Paris was liberated in August and by mid-September American troops reached the Siegfried Line in Germany. Operation MARKET GARDEN began at Arnhem in the same month. Numerous Germans surrendered at Aachen on 21 October. The end of 1944 saw the Battle of the Bulge in the Ardennes.

Children

Complaints were made in March regarding the banning of children from playing ball games on Wedgnock Green. They asked where children could play, reminding people how the Pigwells Common was unavailable since being ploughed.

WCC announced a fund of £5,000 for helping illegitimate children. Warwick spent £325 on them in the previous year and this money was available for immediate financial assistance such as paying the rail fare for children who wanted to return home. An immediate need for teachers and nurses was highlighted. Warwick schools were criticized, especially those where religion seemed more important than cleanliness. Miss Doorly resigned from KHS after the autumn term. She was adamant 'Girls can be wife, mother and careerist.' Girls helped with the harvest and other farming jobs. Her successor was Miss Gwendoline Muriel Wiseman from Christ's Hospital in Hertfordshire. A nursery

Children's Corner, St Nicholas Park. (David Unitt)

opened for forty children in Priory Road, holding its first party at Christmas.

Former Warwick School pupil Major Francis Macaskie was the first British officer to enter liberated Athens. He made three escape bids from Crete. Sentenced to death by the Germans for being a spy, he escaped from the condemned cell.

Warwick School governor Austin Edwards died after a prolonged illness. A former mayor, he had financed the Children's Corner in the Park. A film manufacturer in the Coventry Road, he lived at The Brook, St John's. Another of his many activities had been organizing *Orpheus* which was performed at the Castle. He was also a governor of KHS.

Communications

Henry Thistleton, town crier since 1932, made announcements helped by his bell. Early in 1944, he exchanged the bell for a loudspeaker. When the author was town crier, he never used a loudspeaker.

Several local pupils helped with the post during the Christmas period. In February Private Ray Naylor of the RWR was serving in India when he received an anonymous 21st birthday card from a Warwick girl. He appealed through the *Advertiser* to contact her, but his location was withheld on censorship grounds; however, it could be given to the girl.

In August, Mrs Sneed and her two children, living in Joyce Pool, were listening to the BBC. Imagine their surprise when her husband came on the air from India and sent them all his love. As the year ended there was a biting frost which was well matched by the 'dismal dirge' being played on air. Another patriotic poem followed: 'But they're all British Soldiers, The Salt of the Earth.'

Telegraph poles now came from England instead of abroad and Land Girls helped to identify 17,000 miles of them. Some 2,000,000 poles were already in existence.

Food and Drink

Food

Despite the initial cost and difficulty in setting up, bee-keeping mania swept the country. Keepers were entitled to extra rations of sugar, which was dyed green to prevent human consumption. Farmers were instructed not to spray arsenic insecticide on open blossoms because it killed 90 per cent of bees. William Payne, Lakin Road was fined £20 plus £3 3s advocate's fee and 11s costs for lying about a pig he had bought from John Toney the previous June. It was legal to buy the animal to keep on one's own property, but not to buy it for slaughter at Christmas. Payne paid £5 towards the beast but denied owning it or a sty.

A good harvest was recorded, despite WCC forbidding its employees to help, maintaining that it was too short of staff. Farmers were congratulated by A.C. Mills for their splendid harvest of 70 tons from Warwick Common, despite the weather changing before its completion. PoW working hours were 8.00

am to 6.00 pm including an hour's lunch break Monday to Friday; 8.00 am to 1.00 pm including a half-hour tea break on Saturdays. Local variations applied dependent on the camp commandant. Weekday pay was 9s 6d per day and 5s 6d for Saturdays. Threshing earned an extra 1s per day and 6d on Saturdays. Travel time was included. The Young Farmers' Club reported the growing influence of women in farming. Graham Doughty described powdered potatoes as 'evil, but you ate them or starved.'

Thomas Henry Wood and Margaret Helen Wood, manager and wife of the Wheatsheaf, appeared at the Quarter Sessions. Thomas was charged with stealing and Margaret with receiving seventy-six tins of soup and forty-two of milk. A car was seen at Norton Lindsey with two men emptying cartons into a ditch. The police were informed and recovered the above and discovered the car belonged to Thomas. Next day Inspector Buckley and Detective Constable Saxby were informed about the theft of tinned food from Birmingham. Margaret was interviewed and apparently confessed. Thomas was charged with theft, but he was acquitted at court. Margaret was dismissed. With no independent witnesses, neither spouse was compelled to testify against the other.

Three months into 1944, no decisions had been made about the British Restaurant. The *Advertiser* mentioned many Birmingham cyclists going home disappointed at not finding one. No. 22 Jury Street was finally earmarked and opened after Christmas with eighty-four covers. The cook was Mrs Lewis. Complaints followed about its commodities being purchased from outside Warwick. The manageress Mrs W.J. Tobin replied that she had to obtain supplies from wherever she could. In November the borough treasurer was overwhelmed with complaints regarding the portion sizes (presumably too small). He considered they were unfounded, but the manageress resigned soon afterwards.

Drink

An unknown Warwick pub closed for the whole bank holiday weekend. Harold George Skipp and the Birmingham company who owned the Punchbowl were fined £20 each plus a total of £88 analysts' fees for diluting gin. Arthur Edward Bishop of the Bear and Bacchus was fined £20 for obstructing WCC officers and diluting his gin. Towards the end of the year, landlords were permitted to dilute spirits provided they gave prior notice.

Health

Kenilworth soldier Private Leslie Honey (20) was cycling home along the Coventry Road in the blackout when he was killed by an ambulance driven by Mrs Edith Climson. A witness, William Whittington Jones, Paradise Street, had been overtaken by the ambulance which was close in to the kerb

Coventry Road pre-Pottertons. (Terry Adkins)

and travelling very slowly. Mrs Climson was not blamed for Private Honey's death, the cause of which remained a mystery. St John Ambulance Girl Cadets (Nursing Division) had their flag dedicated in St Mary's.

Henry Norman Bennett (61), Friars Street, died from lumbar pneumonia. A heavy weight dropped on his foot at Emscote Foundry, Emscote Road, confining him to bed where his lung became infected. A verdict of natural causes was recorded. Italian PoW Antonio Salis was crushed to death between two railway trucks. He had been conscripted into the Pioneer Corps, although he did not speak English and did not understand the warning shouted at him. The coroner recorded a verdict of accidental death, adding that where non-English-speaking people were engaged in dangerous jobs, a lookout who spoke the relevant language needed to be employed.

Temporary Police Inspector Robert Wardimans returned home off night duty to Newburgh Crescent and found his wife Elizabeth (42) in a gas-filled room. She had only been back from holiday for two days but was depressed and anxious about the health of their youngest daughter, who was now almost fully recovered. He was helped by Inspector Buckley who lived nearby.

Ronald Charles Lawson (15), Hill Street, was awarded £86 12s 6d plus £15 15s costs from Joseph Lucas & Co., Emscote Road, for the loss of a fingertip. He was allowed £15 for clothes. The rest was invested on his behalf. Lucas were also fined £10. Recipients of false teeth via National Insurance were advised not to sign any paper until they were satisfied with them. Optician Lloyd Averns, Jury Street, asked people who could not keep appointments to let him know. He recommended people to keep a spare pair of spectacles at home.

Red ants returning to Warwick Hospital in February were resistant to insecticides. Chelsea Insecticides of Birmingham guaranteed to remove them, along with mice and black beetles, for 305 guineas per annum. Warwick Division nurses won the Field Cup in the local Ambulance Competition. During the year, Warwick District nurses made 10,000 visits.

The hospital became very busy following D-Day with regular hospital trains arriving. These were painted white with red crosses on them. They unloaded the wounded in the railway sidings normally used for cattle. Here they were received by Red Cross nurses and taken to the hospital. Many had come straight from Europe still wearing bloodstained bandages and dressings. Some were walking wounded, but most were not. Very few ambulances were available and portable beds were used. Once in the hospital, the regular nurses took over. In what is now the main car park, an incinerator burned amputated limbs and dressings, etc. It never went out.

Once they were mobile, wounded patients visited Warwick but had to wear a uniform of blue jacket, trousers, white shirt and red tie. The chief constable disapproved of them wandering around the town so dressed. They were forbidden to enter pubs and their uniforms immediately identified them. Many ignored these orders and entered pubs, where they rarely purchased any drinks as these were bought for them. Others left most of their uniforms in friendly houses. One was rumoured to be a Sikh, complete with a turban, although nobody ever saw him. A plea went out for local drivers to take wounded personnel to events. Many people enrolled as blood donors.

The war going well meant that public toilets were now illuminated at night.

Home Defence

ARP

Air-raids had reduced substantially but if they increased, more ARP staff would be needed. Volunteers relieved some of their counterparts in flying bomb-affected areas in southern England. Specially-trained American troops helped out and came under British control. Conscientious objector Edgar Francis Dobell, 10 Swan Street, was fined £10 for failing to comply with an order directing him to the ARP depot. His defence was 'I can only obey the Law of God, and I would only be a hindrance to others.'

Blackout

Street lights were turned back on in early July, and many people left their curtains open for longer periods. Blackout regulations were relaxed in September. Poor street lighting, now referred to as 'dim-out', in the Market Place was blamed for the death of William Henry Barton, Millers Road, who was killed by a Midland Red bus. Emscote Lawn School advertised a 'well-equipped ARP shelter'.

Civil Defense

The town clerk rejected a request for a CD competition because all organizations were working at full stretch as the country was on high alert. D-Day had just taken place and a week later flying bombs were arriving. Duties were relaxed in September and the CD held a combined exercise in the Square which simulated a bomb blast at the Rock Laundry and Bradshaws Stores with casualties.

On 15 November, Warwickshire County CD strength was drastically reduced:

	Actual Strength	Proposed Strength
Wardens	6,588	3,632
Rescue Parties	1,360	968
Report Control	876	554
Messengers	881	176
First-aid & Ambulance	1,765	639

Evacuees and Refugees

Not all evacuees behaved themselves. In late August two boys from Southam stole a woman's handbag from her bicycle in Banbury Road. The police, assisted by the boys' headmaster Mr Baple (see below), recovered it less £5 7s 4d, a fountain pen and ration book. Mr Baple repaid £2 of the missing money and undertook to obtain the balance from their parents. No further action was taken.

The arrival of flying bombs did not directly affect Warwick, but resulted in an influx of mothers and children from southern

England who needed billets. There remained a mixed reaction to evacuees returning to Warwick. Some people were unwelcoming, possibly with some justification. Yet Mr Baple, headmaster of Banstead Hall School, Banstead, Surrey, was made very welcome. It is unclear whether this was still the case after two of his pupils stole the handbag (see above).

Fire Brigade

The *Advertiser* stated how NFS members from Warwick and Leamington produced 'essential instruments in their leisure'. No other information was given. The RSPCA warned that horses were being burned to death because there were no sacks available to put over their heads when rescuing them. Horses could be led safely through flames provided they could not see them. The NFS nationally accepted female volunteers; twenty-five lost their lives before the war ended.

Water supplies in March were low, although not at danger levels. These worries continued throughout the low rainfall year. In July warning notices were posted about the problem. People were advised not to leave taps running and filling baths to one-third depth was sufficient. It was December before the hosepipe ban was lifted, but economic use of water was still needed.

Fire-watcher Frederick John Samuel Clarke, Peel Road, was fined £2 for missing his duty. Following D-Day, watchers were warned that enemy air-raids could still happen. Oliver Cromwell, Upper Cape was fined £5 plus £2 2s costs for having booked on duty and then found somewhere to sleep. Watchers were stood down from duty in late December. More than 11,380 gas masks were checked in early June.

Home Guard

HG John Toney, 81 Coten End, appeared in court for being absent from duty on several occasions. He had ignored an official warning sent to him by registered letter. Toney argued that he worked seventy-four hours a week looking after 125 assorted cows, pigs and horses. At calving time, he was often up all night and ill health made it difficult for him to work at night. The magistrates still fined him £5 including costs.

Later in the year, members of the HG were given a 'large quantity of eats' and 9 gallons of beer by Miss Peake for their function at the Castle Hill Restaurant. Compulsory drills for the HG were ended. Many HG maintained long-lasting friendships. In expectation of being stood down, Warwick HG joined with Leamington HG for a farewell dinner in the same restaurant. Anthony Eden attended Warwick's stand-down parade on 8 December. Before the year was out, the Warwick branch of HG had formed an Old Comrades' Association.

Law and Order

Crime

Corporal Rhys Evans (24), Glamorgan, dated former nurse Anne Elizabeth Chaplin, maintaining that he was single and wanted to marry her. She agreed and indulged in sexual relations, but whenever they talked about rings, he complained they were too expensive. Finding she was pregnant, the banns were read in Coventry. Suddenly Evans said he had to go on a six-week course and suggested withdrawing them. Meanwhile a wounded sergeant in Warwick Hospital heard about them. He knew that Evans was already married and informed the police. Evans was arrested and went to prison for two years.

In February Phyliss Irene Fry from Glamorgan was fined £5 for unlawfully leaving her employment as a presser in an important job, whose application for release had been refused. She had not worked since 23 December 1943. Next month, Kenneth Hall Kerr, trading as Kresta & Co., Parkes Street, was fined £5. He had failed to notify the factory inspector about an accident in which a worker lost an arm. Miss Marjorie Pickard (20), Parkes Street, was fined £1 for being absent without leave from her employment at Warwick Laundry.

Ex-Squadron Leader Arthur Ernest Masters (50), Broad Street, went to prison for twelve months with hard labour. Masters had raised money and cashed cheques on behalf of the RAF Benevolent Fund, which was in fact his own benevolent fund, and he denied the charge: 'Oh, definitely not guilty.' He had numerous convictions for similar offences. One of his victims was Leonard Toney. Grannies were warned not to be taken in by children calling to say they were going to the cinema, but had forgotten their money and would they pay for them? Nellie Ferguson, now a laundry hand, All Saints Road, was fined £10 or twenty-eight days in prison for embezzling £5 19s 6d whilst employed as a conductress for the Midland Red Omnibus Company.

Two Warwick girls aged 9 and 10 stole evacuee Ruth Elizabeth Lee's handbag. She chased and caught them. Everything was recovered except for 5½d. The girls came from 'a far from ideal home', and were 'very untruthful, disinterested and dishonest'.

Mrs Marion Griffin, Upper Cape, usherette at the New Cinema, alleged she had been attacked with intent to ravish by American Private Hubert C. Harrison. He admitted dating her but denied the allegations. She later confessed to having invented the story and went to prison for six months. Private Francis Bull, Leicestershire Regiment, went to prison for six months for indecently assaulting two small girls on the Common.

Ena May Wilkes from Leamington failed to appear in court for shoplifting. She had been bailed, with her mother standing surety. It was believed she had mental problems and her £5 bail money was not forfeited. She appeared in court a few days later charged with further similar offences, including £32 worth of cigarettes while on bail. Following observations, she was considered fit to plead and went to prison for twelve months.

George J. Mason Ltd, Smith Street, were fined £12 2s on four specimen charges of selling underweight prepacked foodstuffs. It was felt that this was down to carelessness rather than with criminal intent.

Police

Kemble's maximum salary was £1,300 per annum. Police Sergeant William Frederick Homans, now a lieutenant, was posted for duty in Europe with Inspector Gardner from

Kenilworth. Potential female recruits must be unmarried with a minimum height of 5ft 4in and be paid a weekly salary of £2 18s 8d. Uniform, boot and lodging allowances were included. Officers would be required to live away from home.

Leisure and Entertainment

Warwick held a book drive hoping to raise 30,000 books, periodicals, etc. to be given to blitzed libraries. Warwickians were reading more, with a great demand for the classics.

Eagle recreation ground in Hampton Road had a 'Kiddies Day' that included a baseball match between two American teams. It was billed as 'a counter attraction to tennis'. Boxer Dick Turpin returned to the boxing ring after being on active service for two years but was defeated in his first match. Dick was the older brother and trainer of Randolph Turpin, who was regarded as a future champion. Indeed, in 1951 Randolph became World Middleweight Champion when he defeated the legendary Sugar Ray Robinson. Randolph's statue stands in the Square. The Dun Cow fishing club was still causing complaints at the sewage site and faced a threat of being banned. Warwick Police Rifle Club held its first annual dinner at the Castle Hill Restaurant; seventy-two members and eleven ladies were among the attendees. Their application to purchase land in the Packmores for a rifle range was declined. They were later allowed to use the old quarry in Wharf Street. Eagle Engineering sports facilities including tennis, cricket and bowls were available for private members at fees 'which are considered eminently reasonable' [no further details known]. Staff were urged to use the facilities.

This year's carnival included a funfair in the Park. Sally's Gymkhana was held at Myton Hamlet. The All British Amusements Funfair set up in the Park in May, with Galloping Horses, Cake Walk, Over the Sticks, Chairoplanes, Swinging Boats, Children's Roundabouts, Cocoa Nuts [sic] and Houp La [sic]. The Faith for England Pageant was held at St Mary's on the eve of St George's Day (22 April). All town and county parishes were invited to take part.

ENGINEERING IN WARWICK

A MECHANICAL GULLEY AND CESSPIT EMPTIER

A Product of

THE EAGLE ENGINEERING Co., Ltd.

Eagle Engineering. (David Unitt)

Fetes helped to raise money for the 'Salute the Soldier' campaigns. In August the British Legion held one in Warwick Castle grounds. Admission was by the main gate only: adults @ 1s 6d; service personnel @ 1s; children @ 6d but must be accompanied. The event was a success despite bad weather.

A party was arranged by the ARP for children at the tin chapel in Lower Cape and Pickard Street. Children took their own mug and teaspoon, all carefully marked as no spares were available. They went and left early because of the blackout. Parents contributed 6d a week and ration points. Food included jelly and blancmange, pineapple chunks and peaches from South Africa and America.

A dance held at the Warwick Arms in September was by invitation only. Warwick Laundry & Dry Cleaners held a pre-Christmas dance at the Court House. On the same night, the police hired Shire Hall, with all proceeds going to the Police Benevolent Fund. A few nights later, Herbert William Tuffrey from Leamington rescued two girls from being pestered by Davy Drew at a dance in the Court House. Driving home, he collided with a coach in West Street, in which Herbert was one of the passengers. Drew was fined £25 for the driving offence plus £4 17s 7d costs and a further £10 for misuse of petrol.

The WVS staged a concert at St Paul's Canteen, titled 'Six Stars in Battledress'. All performers had been entertainers before the war. A new piano was purchased for the Court House. The RSPCA reminded people that 'pets were not just for Christmas'. Residents at the Warwick Arms were treated to a cup of tea in bed on Christmas Day, served at 7.00 am by committee members.

The entire film *Now, Voyager*, valued at £25, was stolen and rendered useless by a 13-year-old boy from Leamington. It was in a car parked in the County Cinema car park and the boy claimed he had found it. The magistrates sent him to a remand school until he was old enough to be transferred to an approved school.

Eric Coates' new specially-composed *Salute the Soldier* was performed on the wireless by the Stanford Robinson BBC Theatre Orchestra.

As the holiday time approached, people were told in no uncertain terms:

The signal is against Holiday Travel this Easter. [The picture of a railway signal on 'stop' accompanied the notice.]

Do not hinder the transport of men, tanks and shells by taking a journey or adding to the great strain already imposed on the Railways. Don't invade the trains this Easter.

Railway Executive Committee

More than 10,000 people attended the Park events, in good weather.

An *Advertiser* writer known as 'Punch' commented how in the year 2000 the newspapers would be printed on aluminium as the pace of life had become so hot and would have burned paper. Another story involved two bodies being found in Cliffe Hill. One wore no medals, but his identity card described him as a 'Boarder'. He was not very fat, and his occupation was shown as trying to find something to eat. The second was almost as impoverished and described as being a fire-watcher, complete with a certificate from the Married Men's Protection Society giving him a 100 per cent attendance record spent on nights away from home, blitz or no blitz.

Military

America and Canada

Visits by American troops continued, using the Court House and Castle Hill Restaurant for meals. Warwick girls were impressed by the influx of these young men, who were billeted locally. Castle Hill and the Castle Arms became the gathering place for these women, known as 'Yankee Bait', meeting American troops, under the watchful eyes of their military police. Nevertheless, Marion Davies, Millers Road, was fined £2 for obstructing the highway after being warned several times not to do so.

Shortly before D-Day, the local schools were treated to a party at Stoneleigh. Each child was adopted for the day by a GI, given presents and ice cream. Poignantly some GIs gave the last of their English money to the children. They knew they were going abroad and had no guarantee of ever returning. The children gave this money to their parents.

Castle Hill, toilets to left of road off picture. (John Ashbourne)

Reverend Hayden chaired the Hospitality Group and arranged the first lunch for Canadian and others of them. More than 14,000 visiting troops were entertained in this manner.

Army

Corporal Arthur Thomas Giles, Gloucestershire Regiment, was back at home with his parents in Crompton Street after a journey of over 500 miles by boat, train, bullock cart and on foot. On the way, he met and married Marie Eden in India and brought her home to Warwick. Sergeant Sneed, from Joyce Pool, wrote to the *Advertiser* complaining how the 14th Army was regarded as 'The Forgotten Army'.

'Deliverance Day', popularly known as D-Day 1944

The first mention was made in the *Advertiser* of the Allied landings on 9 June and later reported as 'progressing'. The RWR had been on Sword Beach and were fighting at Lebisey Wood, only facing light opposition. By August the Maquis (French Resistance fighters) were 'reported to be doing well in France'.

What is not so well known is the Nazi occupation of Norway tied up 400,000 troops, and effectively stopped them being used against the Allies in Normandy.

Italy

Private Whitehead, All Saints Road, carrier platoon of the Wiltshire Regiment reported: '...then we lined up across the hill and advanced. En route Jerries came out of a ditch behind a tree and when they saw our bayonets, they didn't know which way to go.' Lance Corporal J. Bissell wrote to his wife: 'Imagine my surprise when I was in hospital, I found Wally Wright of Woodhouse Street and Percy Parsons of the Saltisford. The first Warwick chaps I had met since leaving England.' Gunner Arthur Chambers, Wathen Road, died of his wounds after being in action for five weeks.

Merchant Navy

Miss June Wootton, Emscote Road, was made Merchant Navy Queen for the week in September. After being crowned by the Countess of Warwick, the event raised £1,456 4s 7d.

Military Ranges

A warning was issued about the dangers of picking up strange objects on military ranges. Troops were trained 'to kill the enemy, not our own people.' (See 'Health', 1945.)

Prisoners of War: Allied

Relatives of men and women who were casualties, dead, missing or PoWs were asked to give details, and a photograph if possible, to the *Advertiser* for publication free of charge. Escaped PoW Lance Corporal Bissell, Hampshire Regiment, said: 'Jerry was quite decent.' Before the war, he had been a plumber with A. Tandy, Swan Street. Another escaped PoW was Driver Robert

(Bob) Henry Bromwich, RASC, who was captured at Tobruk and now enjoying the comparative freedom of Switzerland, where he was interned. Royal Scots Fusilier Robert G. Colbourne, son of Councillor and Mrs R.B. Colbourne, Cliffe Hill, reported missing in February, was now confirmed as a PoW.

London evacuee Mrs Mary Rosalee McCarthy, Smith Street, appeared in court for stealing £311 when she worked for the RWR headquarters, £206 of which had been repaid. She collapsed when sentenced to four months in prison. Some of the stolen money came from the PoW fund. The magistrates criticized her employers' auditing system. Following the invasion of France, parcels could not be sent to PoWs because of the chaotic state of the railways.

Mrs Mary Nelson was tasked with finding hostesses for the repatriated Dominion PoWs. [Possibly 'hostesses' would not be the most appropriate word to use today.] Repatriated PoWs could not thank the Red Cross enough for all their help. Once back in England, they were visited regularly and offered help if needed.

Prisoners of War: Italian

A letter was published in the *Advertiser* complaining about the influx and generous treatment of Italian PoWs. The writer contrasted this with the harsh treatment some had received in Italy and cited a woman who refused to give water to an injured Allied soldier.

There were two types of PoWs in Warwick: those who co-operated and those who did not. Several hundred co-operative ones were housed on the Common including the old Tote building, which local children were prone to break into. PoWs were allowed within a 5-mile radius of the camp without escort. They could visit the cinema, shops, Post Office, make phone calls and enter any house where they were invited, but not enter pubs, attend dances or use public transport and had to be back at camp by 10.00 pm.

They were very generous to children and on one occasion gave them a large quantity of prunes and a bucket of custard. Some worked on the roads, in the Nelson Dale factory and also to helped erect prefabs (prefabricated homes intended as temporary replacement housing).

Queen Alexandra's Royal Army Nursing Corps (QARANC)

With origins going back to Florence Nightingale, the QAs, as they were called, were established by Royal Warrant in 1902. Since then, its members have been at the forefront of dealing with military casualties wherever campaigns were in progress. It was not a safe occupation. The author had an aunt, Anne Cross, who was a member and spent much of her time in the Middle East.

Nursing Sister Ethel Annie Norbury from Coventry stayed with her brother and sister-in-law at the Nelson Inn, Emscote Road while on leave. She had been in the Corps for three and a

Mrs Anne Cross, Queen Alexandra's Royal Army Nursing Corps. (Author's collection)

half years. During this time, she helped evacuating troops from Dunkirk and had been torpedoed.

Royal Air Force

The County of Warwick Auxiliary Squadron claimed its 100th enemy aircraft shot down. They later shot down seventy-five flying bombs in southern England. Reported missing in July 1943, Sergeant Air Gunner James Henry Thornton, Parkes Street was now confirmed as killed. The author's father's time in Europe is shown on the Christmas card he sent home.

Royal Navy

HMS *Warwick* was sunk off Trevose Head, Cornwall, losing more than half her crew. Able Seaman Norman Mancini (17), Lyttleton Road, enjoyed life in Canada after being shipwrecked.

Royal Warwickshire Regiment

WBC awarded the Freedom of Warwick to the RWR.

Warwickshire Yeomanry

Lieutenant Colonel Guy Jackson, DSO, led an attack which helped the 9th Armoured Division to smash German gun

Author's father's Christmas card, 1944. (Author's collection)

Warwickshire Yeomanry in Italy, now mechanized. (Warwickshire Yeomanry Museum Trust)

positions at El Alamein. Later that year, he lost both feet when he trod on a mine in Italy while on a partridge shoot. Two sergeants who were with him each lost a foot. Rumours about disbandment were denied and, even if true, it would not happen until after the war. In December members came home to a rousing reception and a special service at St Mary's attended by their families and other important guests. It was followed by a parade led by Lieutenant Colonel Lakin.

Rationing and Salvage

Rationing

Every 5lb of coal saved in 40,000 homes provided enough fuel to build a Churchill tank. Coal roundsman Arthur Canning,

Warwickshire Yeomanry returning at Milverton Station. (Warwickshire Yeomanry Museum Trust)

Pickard Row received three months' imprisonment for charging 3s 3d per cwt for coal when the correct price was 2s 9½d.

Social

King George VI called for 3 September to be a day of prayer.

Forty bell-ringers practised in St Mary's. The ban on church bells being rung had gradually been lifted as the threat of invasion lessened, but not be completely removed until after D-Day. Canon Russell left in September, being succeeded by Canon H.D. Lyttler MA from Shipston-on-Stour. The Reverend L.G. Coates, curate, complained about women with rouged lips taking communion and demanded legislation to cease this practice. He received very little support. The Reverend C.J. Passey, Stratford

Warwickshire Yeomanry Parade, Lieutenant Colonel J. Lakin. (Warwickshire Yeomanry Museum Trust)

Road, retorted that all he had to do was to wipe the chalice with a cloth after each parishioner had sipped the wine. Coates was later moved to Upton-with-Skilgate in Somerset. Had he upset too many people? The Bishop of Coventry preached at the Remembrance Day service.

Walter John Tandy was awarded the Royal Humane Society Certificate for saving a 5-year-old child from drowning in the canal. In 1900, his grandfather Thomas Tandy had received a similar award for an identical rescue of a boy from the same canal. An unknown woman donated money to purchase cigarettes for wounded British and Canadian soldiers.

The British Legion was making plans for demobilization and hoped the war would end in Europe during the year. Japan was not mentioned. At the same time, the military stopped discharging wounded soldiers before they had completed their medical treatment. Once again, concern was raised regarding how small shops would fare during this period with all the restrictions and regulations they faced in addition to competition from their larger rivals. A meeting in the Court House endorsed the activities of WBC against combines, multiple and chain stores, co-ops and bureaucracy. The mayor felt that Warwick shops did not have the pull of the larger towns. Advice was available to employers regarding post-war employment.

Following D-Day, women in Britain were asked by the government to help clothe the children of Occupied Europe. It was a massive problem as the factories were unable to cope with the high demand from home and abroad. Many knitters were needed.

As no building land was currently available in the town centre, the removal of the museum was recommended along with bringing Hampton-on-the-Hill and Budbrooke into the borough; widening Castle Lane for a shopping mall to be built between there and Jury Street and High Street. [It is uncertain how this would fit in with Lord Derby's plan to develop the UK for tourism.] There was strong opposition to the suggested demolition of the museum: 'Now that Warwick has been mercifully spared from enemy bombs, we should indeed place more value than ever on our historic buildings.'

The Bishop of Coventry, Dr Neville Gorton, preached a scathing attack on Warwick housing, arguing how many houses should be condemned. He stressed that housing was a matter for the community, the churches and WBC. The council objected to his attack, having built 608 houses in the past twenty-five years. More comments followed from home and abroad. A lack of houses for workers was blamed for so little business involvement in the area.

Public washing baths were recommended and The Warwick Stores, 7 Smith Street, offered to remake mattresses with local ones being returned the same day. WBC recorded the shortest council meeting in January, which lasted just one minute.

The Mop Fair raised £61 1s 6d for the mayor's Hospital Fund. These reported record takings gave rise to the comment: 'This is not surprising when we recall that 1s was charged for a few turns on the big wheel.'

St John's Brook needed to be rat de-infested at a cost of £15. WBC agreed to share the services of a regular rat operative with Leamington for £4 5s per week. More action was taken: 'RAT MENACE in Warwick and District. Every man, woman and child is asked to be a Rat Reporter', completing a coupon from the *Advertiser* or posting a card to Pageant House or Waterloo Place in Leamington whenever a rat was seen.

Mop Fair. (Author's collection)

Ex-RAC repatriated Corporal Cecil George Aldred, eldest son of William and Laura Aldred, Brook Street, married Doris Cooper from Colwyn Bay at St Nicholas. His best man was ex-RWR repatriated Private Frank Ball. They had met as PoWs in Germany. After a honeymoon in Colwyn Bay, the newlyweds lived in Kenilworth. Royal Canadian Air Force Flying Officer Richard Bishop, Moose Jaw, Saskatchewan, married Margaret Joan Thornton, Parkes Street. The couple honeymooned in southern England and would return to Canada in due course. 'The bride wore a brown tailored bird's eye flecked suit and accessories to match.'

Warwick WI was praised for the work they did. Fresh training was arranged for the WVS regarding the increased risks of air-raids when the invasion of Europe started. Training was given by Mr Todd, ARP first-aid and rescue officer. Members helped raise funds for 'Salute the Soldier' week. Soon afterwards they appealed for 'anything for Londoners' to use in face of the latest air-raids. This appeal continued into 1945 and commented that Kenilworth had already sent 7 tons of goods to Shoreditch. Mrs T.H. Ryland, co-organizer of the WVS and vice chairman of the WI, reported how the government relied on the ladies in general 'and had never found them wanting.' The county office was at 6 Northgate Street.

Transport

No special bus services were run over Easter to save rubber and petrol. Motor cyclist Frank Parker Jeffs, Church Road, Claverdon, was killed in late July in Hampton Road when he collided with a Stratford Blue bus driven by Percy Goode. A verdict of 'Accidental Death' was recorded. In December buses were asked not to drive over the pavement at the junction with Castle Street and Jury Street. Complaints were made about Stratford Blue buses not picking up passengers when requested between Warwick and Leamington.

Coventry lorry driver Arthur Frederick Watts was fined £3 and his licence endorsed for speeding and racing. He told the court how he 'likes to get a move on and doesn't like to be passed by American Army Jeeps.'

A New Year appeal was made for part-time workers on the railways in the Warwick and Leamington area at weekends offering 'good rates of pay'. Another plea followed in June: 'If you must travel, travel light.' Mrs Lillian Goodhew (29), St Nicholas Church Street, a porteress [as reported in the *Advertiser*] at Warwick Station, was bound over for twelve months with £2 5s costs for stealing a blouse from a suitcase. Later in the year she admitted an earlier similar theft of clothes from the station. A twelve-month probation order was added to her previous sentence, plus £2 compensation.

Serious thought was given nationally about the construction of motorways post-war by commercial, industrial concerns and the British Road Federation.

CHAPTER TEN

Victory: 1945

During March, the Allies established a bridge over the Rhine at Remagen. During the following month, Buchenwald and Belsen concentration camps were liberated and Hitler committed suicide. All German forces surrendered unconditionally on 7 May and VE (Victory in Europe) Day, as it became known, was celebrated on the 8th. A change of government resulted in Clement Attlee succeeding Churchill as prime minister on 26 July. Atomic bombs were dropped on Hiroshima and Nagasaki in August, soon to be followed by the Japanese surrender and VJ (Victory over Japan) Day was declared on 2 September. On 24 October, the United Nations organization was created. The Nuremburg war crimes trials began.

Children

Gilbert Farnfield's daughter married in India and he was buried at Milverton in early May. The Reverend Hayden, an old friend, assisted. By June, no name appeared as headmaster of Emscote Lawn. In August the school advertised as preparing pupils for public schools and the RN. The third Warwick Youth Week ended with a sports day at the Eagle recreation ground.

Communications

VE Day saw the end of the ban on church bells being rung. Regardless of the theatre of war, the cost of postage rose to

1½d for all letters up to 1oz in weight. Only one postal delivery was made on Whit Monday and the counter closed at noon. An advert from 1918 was re-vamped: 'There will be a terrible day of reckoning for Germany which has placed herself outside the family of Nations by her inhumanity and shamelessness.'

Food and Drink

Food

Following VE Day, Warwick held a 'Welfare Foods' week, stressing the importance of a balanced diet for children. The end of the war did not mean the return of ample food supplies, and growing your own was still actively promoted: 'An hour in the garden saves one in the queue.' Joseph Rouse (no known address) and John Ernest Giles, Newburgh Crescent, appeared in court for stealing poultry from the Common. A grinning Rouse was given six months' imprisonment and Giles four months'. Rouse was a regular offender and in 1947 involved some German PoWs in his crimes.

The idea of paying PoWs by the hour was not popular, especially if the transport was late in arriving. A suggestion to use German PoWs on the land was not well received. Farmers were instructed not to pay PoWs or give them any other rewards. These all had to be sent to the PoW camp.

By March, the British Restaurant was classed as a success. Main meals cost 1s and tea 1½d. However, the parsimonious Ministry of Food would not authorize the spending of £100 on toilet facilities!

Drink

The ratio of population in Warwick was 236 people to every pub. Harold Skipp applied for the renewal of his licence but was warned by the magistrates about diluting gin. It was permissible, provided due notice had been given, although Allied forces in the town felt that they had been robbed. Yeoman Walker & Co., Liverpool, were fined £5 for wrongly labelling lemon juice as

British Restaurant. (Public domain)

such when it contained a substitute. Mellor & Co. were fined £2 plus £3 3s costs for selling cordial which lacked sugar.

Health

The headless body of a man on the railway line by the station in January was identified as George Charles Harold Newton (67), a retired draper from Leamington. Joseph Henry Blakeman, Edward Street, was found dead in his lorry at the Corn Stores in St Nicholas Church Street. His lorry had stalled and jerked him forward and the resulting whiplash broke his neck. Sapper William Henry Clarke was killed at Budbrooke when a petrol drum fell on him.

In February, Stanley Llewellyn, Wathen Road was killed on Wedgnock Rifle Range and Reginald Holland, Peel Road and Eric Powell, Parkes Street were seriously injured. Ronald Sanger, Lyttleton Road, escaped unhurt when an unexploded device detonated. [The author went very cold when he discovered this tale. Literally only a couple of years after VJ Day he used to play up on the same range, with all sorts of strange but very interesting objects lying around. He was very lucky.] (See 'Military' 1944 above.)

Later in February, Doris May Woodfield (22), Peel Road, was found in the Avon at Hampton Lucy, having been missing since the previous November. When told by her father not to be late home or she would be locked out, Doris replied she would jump in the river if that happened. Tragically he had not believed her. The coroner said he would leave it to her father's conscience regarding his locking her out.

After being cleansed, 32 Brook Street had the Scabies Order that had been in force on the premises removed. Following VE Day, WBC disagreed with WCC's comments regarding publicity about venereal disease. WBC maintained that they already had sufficient advertisements in place. Once it was recognized as a countywide problem, WBC was 'happy to assist'. WCC paid 9s per week for a limited number of children to receive surgery for defective eyesight. Land under Emscote Road railway bridge was earmarked for public toilets.

WCC praised the local wartime nurses who were 20 per cent under strength, which caused problems treating patients with TB in Coventry and Warwickshire. The Warwickshire Red Cross treated sick and wounded patients to a tea and pianoforte recital at Shire Hall. Nurses and patients enjoyed the dancing, including those with wounded legs. L.J. Smith, Coten End and a repatriated PoW wrote to the *Advertiser* praising the work of the Red Cross and St John Ambulance: 'We alone realise fully your help.'

General Stanislav Bosy, Czechoslovak Military Mission, visited Warwick Hospital and presented staff with the Czechoslovakian Medal for Merit for their treatment of his fellow countrymen. Aero Engine Rootes Securities raised £300 from the sale of surplus stock and purchased a 'talkie cinematograph' for the patients. As many patients as possible were sent home for Christmas.

Home Defence

The CD was disbanded on 2 May and its social centre moved to the Court House. A farewell parade was held in Hyde Park in June before King George VI. Representatives attended from all over the country. The evacuee scheme ended in April, but many children had already returned home. All unwanted static water tanks were removed by the NFS, which reverted to its pre-war status. Nobody knew what would happen to gas masks. Following VE Day, their disposal began.

Law and Order

Crime

Captain Guy S. Glover, RWR, brother of Virginia Sabreton, wife of Reverend Sabreton at All Saints, was murdered by John Mavity, a repatriated PoW in Handsworth, Birmingham. Guy was the nephew of Mr and Mrs W.J. Glover, Fieldhead, Myton Road and Mavity's former commanding officer. Mavity was found guilty but insane at Birmingham Assizes and detained for life.

Reginald Charles Pheasey, stoker at Warwick Gas Works, threw a knife at his daughter Doris when she refused to give him any money. While lucky not to lose an eye, she spent seven days in hospital. He went to prison for four months and his five children were taken into the care of WCC.

Avril Eaton Winslow (29), a nurse at Warwick Hospital, bigamously married William Melville Bristow of the Royal Canadian Air Force. She fainted in the dock on receiving a twelve-month prison sentence. Private Harry Atkinson, Pioneer Corps, from Wakefield received a twenty-one-month prison sentence for bigamously marrying Olive Mildred Montague. When sentenced, he was already in prison for being absent without official leave.

Laurence Arthur Malin (20), Greville Road, appeared in court again for refusing to work, claiming he was too self-conscious because of a maimed hand to work in a factory. In 1943 he had agreed 'to lead an honest and industrious life for two years, and go to work.' His comments were not a good enough excuse for not going to work and he was committed to the Quarter Sessions with a view to sending him to Borstal. Within a matter of days, he started work.

Lance Corporal Victor Bert Harris of the Military Police was fined £5 for indecently exposing himself in Chapel Street. Damage was caused to toilets on Castle Hill. John Toney was fined £2 for being drunk and disorderly at 81 Coten End. A new-condition gent's Swallow raincoat was lost or stolen from the WCC car park on North Rock; an unspecified reward was offered for its return.

George Sydney Smith (62), storeman at the territorial Air Force stores in the Museum and co-defendant Walter Shearsby (22), a sheet metal worker, were fined £10 for stealing military equipment from the store. Both men came from Whitnash.

Discharged airman William Presley Bissett from Chiswick was fined £5 or one month in prison for unlawfully wearing the Distinguished Flying Cross medal. He received a further four months for stealing a tea boiler and a suitcase.

The Social Committee of the Warwick Arms Social Committee agreed to recompense members of staff who had been robbed by the chef.

Police

PWR Frederick William London, Broad Street, was killed when he fell off a ladder while cleaning windows at the rear of his house. In August PWR Harry Stretton indicated that he would resign the day after the Japanese surrendered, having served for forty-five years in the police. Harry joined in 1900 after serving in the Second Boer War and retired in 1925, having seen service in the Great War. He resumed duties in 1926 at the time of the General Strike and again in May 1939.

Not all forces used policewomen during the war but needed to do so afterwards. Some chiefs wrote to Kemble asking for his opinion. He was effusive in his praise, in complete contrast to his earlier opposition.

Leisure and Entertainment

Mobile libraries were towed by army transport units. Warwick took part in the national WVS Victory Book Drive to provide 3,000,000 books for armed service personnel stationed abroad.

Following VE Day, the boats for hire on the Avon were inspected and found to be leaking and unsafe. Provided hirers did not mind bailing water out, they could have them for 1s. Warwick's first dinghy race was cancelled because of bad weather. Warwick darts players, including women, were considered 'a fine body of sportsmen'. The Dun Cow fishing club continued causing damage and their application to continue using the site was deferred. A team of women beat a team of men on the Common in a tug-of-war. The men's excuse for losing was that they were frightened to pull too hard against the women!

The carnival was cancelled, blaming a disappointing response, but VE Day had recently happened and people were probably more interested in street parties. Butlins advertised that their Luxury Camp in Filey, Yorkshire, was remaining open until the end of October. No one anticipated how Holocaust victims would react to this. They could only equate any camp with concentration camps and thought they were being returned to such horrors.

A group advertised as 'The Don Cossack Riders – The Fearless Horsemen' performed in Myton Fields on 22 June, presenting a programme of 'daring and death-defying feats'; adults @ 2s, children @ 1s. In August the Rosaire Family Circus came to the Park. The event included the Grand Hercules Cycle Competition and offered £50 in prizes. [No other details known.]

The Chamber of Commerce held their first dinner since 1922. Their objective was to keep Warwick on the map. After VE Day the Ambulance First-Aid Service held a final supper. Wartime austerity and sobriety continued. Shops had no stocks. Patients in Warwick Hospital who were unable to go home had their wards decorated with Christmas trees, holly, mistletoe and paper chains. Dinner was turkey, sprouts, roast potatoes, mince pies and plum pudding. Nurses added to the festivity by wearing their cloaks inside out and showing the red linings. Local girls complained about a lack of dances in Warwick and having to go to Leamington for them. They felt there should be a minimum of five dance halls in Warwick. Their views were supported by the soldiers billeted in the locality.

Humour – Topical Jokes

Hitler and Himmler were disguised as women trying to escape from Germany. They went into a bar where they were recognized by the barman. 'How did you recognize us?' asked Hitler. 'Because I'm Goebbels,' he replied.

Warwick girls coming out of the services were asked by the demobilization officer 'What was your profession before enlisting?' Reply: 'None. Well off.' Demobilization officer: 'Right…a nunnery for you.' [Not very amusing today, but a different sense of humour in those days.]

An RWR sergeant instructor in the Middle East reported on the problems teaching English while suffering from a cold. Asking 'Do you know anything about Shakespeare?' he received the answer: 'No, we know lager beer, and bass beer but never Shakesbeer.'

VE Day

There were great celebrations for VE Day, with flags and bunting encouraged everywhere, much of it purchased by WBC.

The author was on the back of his mother's bicycle in Leamington and had been given a Union Jack to wave but did not understand why. Bored with waving it, he put the flag down in between the spokes of the bicycle's rear wheel…not a good idea! Impromptu church services were held everywhere with bells ringing, open-air dancing and pubs staying open until 11.30 pm. The *Advertiser* quoted: 'Men and women of all the Services wheeled and turned and accomplished all manner of acrobatics that pass for dancing among you moderns…flirted discreetly in the shadows.'

The mayor and councillors attended a non-denominational church service in the Castle courtyard next day. On the first Sunday after VE Day, churches were filled with people giving thanks and there was a great welcome ringing of bells.

Street Parties

The Transport Commission had to be involved in all street parties, initially for VE and later for VJ Days. VE Day tended to be mainly quiet, mindful that the war was still being fought against Japan, but street parties still took place in defiance of the weather. Tables were tastefully and abundantly laden.

With the Japanese surrender, the world moved from war to peace. When the mayor announced the surrender there was dancing in the Square until 4.00 am, which he led. A Thanksgiving Service was held at St Mary's and all the other churches. These were followed by street parties in Lyttleton Road and elsewhere. Children were given goody bags and 1s. The day ended with bonfires and fireworks. More parties were held in the following days. Yet at the same time, people were being admitted to Warwick Hospital suffering from malnutrition and a plea was made for fresh eggs. Another party was held in Lyttleton Road in September for twenty-five children organized by their parents, ending with music and dancing.

Coten End School closed for two days following VE Day. The attendance was very poor when it re-opened because children had been kept up late celebrating.

Lyttleton Road Party (Pamela Westlake)

Military

The RSPCA advised returning service personnel not to bring exotic pets home because of the problems they would cause.

Mrs Mary Nelson arranged places for returning troops who needed rest and recuperation. They invariably arrived at Leamington by train and were often stressed, tearful and sometimes drunk. She found suitable places and hosts to look after them, regardless of their nationality. Some were taken back to her flat at the Nelson Dale works.

Army

Soldiers abroad were unimpressed by having their rations cut by 12.5 per cent.

Americans

Their visits continued and were much appreciated. A young married woman from Parkes Street, who associated openly with Americans, had her application for maintenance from her estranged husband turned down. Peggy Alma Blanche Morgan, Bishop's Itchington, was on Castle Hill with an American. Looking very unkempt, she was asked by the police for her identity card. Unable to produce it, she gave the name of Peggy Cooper, Tachbrook Road, Leamington. Once her true identity had been established, she was charged with using a false name. Blanche failed to appear at court. She had been dismissed from the WAAF for regularly being absent without official leave.

Canadians

At the end of the war, every Warwick child took an empty jam jar to school where it was filled with chocolate powder from Canada. Graham Doughty confessed that not much of it arrived at home!

Banbury Road Toll House, German PoW camp to left hand side of picture.
(Andy Wing)

Prisoners of War: Allied

Private Burton, son of Mr and Mrs Burton, Wharf Street described his treatment as 'pretty terrible' in Stalag XXA, being fed when the guards felt like it. Meals were soup with one or two pieces of bread and the occasional portion of margarine. 'The Red Cross parcels were our salvation.' His memories were supported by Flight Sergeant Derrick Gordon Bicknell, Charles Street. Initially he was in Fallingbostel, near Hanover, until forced to march 80 miles in ten days. They were fed small potatoes and ersatz coffee, which they sometimes managed to heat. Ultimately they were rescued by 'Monty's Boys' and flown back home. His view was shared by many: 'The only good German is a dead one... It will take years to stamp out Nazi education in schools.' Repatriating PoWs was a joint RAF and USAAF operation.

The mayor planned a reception for returning PoWs, appealing for £250 for this purpose. He and his wife shook the PoWs' hands and treated them to sandwiches and drinks. Most PoWs were back in Warwick by the end of May and were treated to a 'welcome home' function a few days later in the Court House. It was described as '...one of the brightest gestures of hospitality that the old town has made for a long time.' All services, military and civil, were involved and the Gaiety Café in Leamington provided cold chicken, tongue and trifle. Jan Berenska played the music and each PoW was given an envelope containing five crisp, new £1 Bank of England notes. Many thanks were given for the support they had received from the Red Cross and St John Ambulance.

A raffle was held in the Park in August to raise £1,500 for the mayor's 'welcome home' fund but it was not successful. Many businesses had not responded and were criticized for being 'quick to forget'. A few weeks later, a successful bazaar at the Court House brought the total to almost £750. By late October, Mrs Pearson heard that her son, Trooper Harold (Daisy) Pearson, who had been a prisoner of the Japanese for three and a half years, was safely in Australia and would be coming home soon.

Prisoners of War: German

Their camp was on the Banbury Road, almost opposite the old toll house, and they were more restricted than the Italians. At some stage they were also on the Common. Others were on working parties in the Myton Road. The camp was demolished in 1947.

A young Graham Doughty came off his bicycle by the PoW camp. Instead of going to Warwick Hospital, he was taken into the camp and treated by a German doctor, who did a good job on him.

In September, Coroner J.H. Tibbits held an inquest into the death of German PoW Jacob Hoffman from the camp at Maxstoke. Along with other PoWs he was in a working party on a lorry driven by Driver Roy Stanley Hubbard (17) along the Warwick-Birmingham Road. Hubbard drove too quickly, and Hoffman was killed when the lorry overturned. At the end of the inquest, German Sergeant Major Heinz Hoppe thanked the

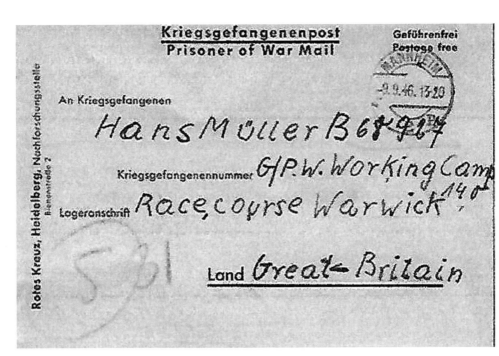

PoW label. (Andy Wing)

coroner for the 'very fair conduct of the enquiry'. A report was sent to Hoffman's parents.

Prisoners of War: Italians

During their captivity, nine PoWs died and were buried in Warwick Cemetery. Eight of them were repatriated later, each body being treated with respect and having a priest in attendance.

Royal Air Force

Police Constable Cleaver, Emscote Road, had been in the RAF for three years and was awarded the OBE. RAF Warwick was situated off the Stratford Road on land owned by the Earl of Warwick and used for training and emergency landings. The last reminders of it have now all gone.

Royal Warwickshire Regiment

The first wedding was reported happening in the Regimental Chapel at St Mary's between Lieutenant Peter Raymond Phillips RWR and Joan Evelyn Shepherd from Birmingham. This claim was disputed by Canon Russell who had previously used the chapel for a marriage and christening. The regiment marched through Warwick with band playing, colours flying and bayonets fixed.

Monty and Enoch Powell

Bernard Law Montgomery, Viscount Alamein, became an officer in the RWR in 1908 and was wounded at Ypres. A forward-thinking soldier, he concentrated on training in preference to drill. His ideas paid dividends during the retreat to Dunkirk and his ultimate success against Rommel. He was chosen as the field commander for the D-Day landings. Monty, as he was fondly known, took the German forces' surrender at Lüneburg Heath on 4 May 1945. The same year Warwick became the first town to make him a Freeman of the Borough. His banner hangs in St Mary's.

Monty. (Author's collection)

Manfred Rommel, son of Erwin Rommel who was Monty's chief opponent in Africa, told the world the true facts behind his father's so-called suicide. In time he and David Montgomery, Monty's son, became good friends.

Another well-known member of the RWR during this time was John Enoch Powell, a controversial MP. His funeral was at St Mary's and he is buried in Warwick.

Rationing and Salvage

Rationing

The Warwick Cinderella Fund founded in 1885 provided serviceable footwear to local children. A.C. Mills agreed that

Funeral of John Enoch Powell, 1998. (Author's collection)

coal miners attracting extortionate prices would affect post-war recovery. Later in the year, coal was rationed from May to October at 20cwt, with the instruction not to burn any of it unless necessary but 'to save it for the winter'. Housewives in June were unimpressed when more reductions in food were introduced because supplies were being sent to Germany and the liberated countries of North-West Europe. 'Victory equalled less food.'

Salvage

Following VE Day, a display in the Court House showed how scrap paper was used for surgical bowls, medical supplies, and parts for aircraft and guns. Visitors were reminded that more was needed to help defeat Japan.

Social

A whist drive of seventy tables raised £24 for the Sunshine Home for Blind Babies in Leamington, while £245 4s 4d was raised for St Dunstan's. Another 'Salute the Soldier' event held in October was the final one of the war. Various entertainments were arranged in the hope of raising £307,000. Half was raised by the middle of the week. The British Legion urgently needed poppy-sellers in the run-up to Remembrance Day. Corporate rates were to be 13s, an increase of 1s 8d.

WCC advised it had no statutory requirement to keep jobs open for service personnel who stayed on after their demobilization date. At the same time, it had a great need of staff. Since VJ Day, many women left their factory employment and returned to domestic service. It was reported how housewives should now not have any difficulty in finding home helps.

Throughout the war, the gelatine works of Nelson Dale in Wharf Street continued working. Gelatine was needed for food and for films. The production process requires animal skins and bones among other items. These were brought in by train and taken into Nelson Lane to be treated. The smell was incredibly vile and the author remembers it well in the 1950s.

The Venerable Algernon Ward, Archdeacon of Warwick, praised the work of the lay preachers in the parish. John H. Tibbits, Old Square, supported the move to have the carillons working again in St Mary's bell tower. They were last heard in the 1890s and he believed 'Warwickshire Lads and Lassies', the regimental march of the RWR, must be restored. Financial support quickly followed. The Reverend Hayden's daughter Josephine became engaged to Francis Farley from London. Mr and Mrs H.M. de Borde's child was christened in the Lord Leycester Hospital chapel by Dr F.N. Frankland, Master. One godparent was the mayor, and a tea party was held at the Court House.

The St John's rat removal operation was repeated at the same price of £15. The knackers' yard at Myton was reported as being 'rat infested'. Public money was being wasted because rest centres were both rat- and moth-infested.

Anthony Eden's election campaign was supported by a surprise visit from Winston Churchill to Leamington. It must have worked because he had a majority of 17,364, although

Winston Churchill in Leamington. (Warwickshire Constabulary History Society)

Winston's Conservative party lost to Labour under Clement Attlee. Sadly, Eden's eldest son was killed in Burma.

Warwick was 'deeply moved' by Franklin Delano Roosevelt's death in April. Flags at the Court House were flown at half-mast. Sunday's service at St Mary's was almost full of members of the public, military, police and American service personnel.

The scouts and guides lit VE Day celebratory camp fires in the Park, and restored the turf afterwards.

Post-War Proposals

The Ministry of Health was asked to provide thirty-nine temporary factory-made houses. Alderman Holmes criticized the plan, saying that there were 4,038 empty houses in Warwick and a quarter of them served no use except for landlords. New houses were not needed for returning servicemen because they already had homes. B. Charlett, Charles Street retorted: 'Some of the more unfortunate have been waiting for more than five years for any kind of home of their own.' Councillor Wallwin supported the need for new houses but suggested brick buildings were preferable to prefabricated.

WBC needed land for 600 houses on the Pigwells Common and built a route between Coventry and Cape Roads. The idea was initially overwhelmingly approved, although Cape residents were concerned about proposed building on Cape Common. Objections followed regarding the Pigwells plans, including government interference. The issue was discussed in the House of Commons and it was agreed that the Common should remain as such. Absentee Councillor Captain E.G. Tibbits opposed the idea of building houses on the Pigwells. More objections followed.

Buildings considered unsafe before the war, situated at the top of the Square and Old Square, were to be demolished for the current WCC Shire Hall offices. This decision had been made before the war. Concern was raised about how many houses could bypass clearance orders, adding that multi-occupancy by two or more families was not ideal. Only 43.5 per cent of 1,760 houses inspected had bathrooms, highlighting the need for public baths.

The Forbes Estate between the Stratford Road and Hampton Road covered 55 acres and was built post-war, including shops and a school. A.C. Mills added his comments. He maintained that the idea of children needing back gardens would be unpopular with the 'house proud' because of the risk of dirt, and 'Who desires a house built near gas works?' His tirade continued: 'Why has land that cattle graze upon become more valuable when it is required to build houses for human beings?'

Sir Patrick Abercrombie was paid £1,000 to re-plan Warwick. In brief, his idea was to knock down all the old buildings, replace them and turn the town into a large shopping centre. Fortunately he was ignored, and Warwick survived. A plan to remove the monument in the Square was opposed, although it would later be removed.

The WVS recorded their numerous activities which included running St Paul's canteen; selling savings certificates; mutual help for housewives; catering for refugees; taking charge of evacuated children; operating mobile canteens for HG and whenever needed, such as at processions, etc.; assisting the Red Cross; collecting blood donor details; sending blankets overseas; and being a fund of information. In addition to repairing soldiers' socks and hospital uniforms, they made holders for Commandos' daggers.

By March they were offering a two-year contract for staff to work overseas and help run the Navy, Army and Air Force Institutes (NAAFI) leave clubs and other welfare work. A thanksgiving service was held for them at St Mary's. The government expressed a need for them to continue for at least the next two years. The WVS pleaded for more woollens to go to Holland: girls' jumpers for 8 to 10-year-olds; jerseys for 2 to 4-year-olds; and shawls for babies. Some 7,000 had already been supplied, but many more were needed.

In February, snowballers aimed for lit windows in Smith Street. Bad weather affected the collection of salvage. During this period, WBC properties reported 196 burst pipes; other owned properties had 550. After VE Day troops were entertained in the Castle, despite the rain. Likewise, rain did not put a dampener on Monty's visit in October.

Transport

Discussions took place about siting an airfield in the Leamington, Warwick and Stratford area. The Stratford Road site was turned down as being too small and would be needed for building purposes.

Private Alphonse Thyssen was fined 15s for not having any lights on his bicycle. He maintained he could only speak American and not English!

Midland Red driver Clifford Birch, Oldbury, put his bus and wounded soldier passengers in a ditch on the Birmingham Road. He was fined £5 for driving without due care and being drunk

Monument in Market Place. (John Ashbourne)

Post-war traffic in High Street and Jury Street. (Author's collection)

plus £1 11s 6d costs and his licence was endorsed. Following VE Day, a request was made to restore the Cape Road bus service. A complaint was made in November about a driver and conductress agreeing not to stop at Guy Street until they had to. Then they let one passenger on board. Following remonstrations from other passengers, she replied 'We're running late', adding that she was 'fed up'. It was necessary to remind the Midland Red that the Packmores service was for the benefit of residents, not the drivers. People who complained were threatened with being turned off the bus.

Warwick roads were being damaged by tractors. A Road Safety campaign started in November. Private William George Taylor, Birmingham, was killed in the Birmingham Road near the Dun Cow. Contrary to military instructions, he walked in the road on the way back to Budbrooke Barracks instead of using the pavement. Taxi driver Edward Price was travelling in the same direction. Nearing the railway bridge, he overtook two cyclists, causing an oncoming motor car driven by Eric

Roy Cole to pull further into his nearside, hitting George. Eric was absolved of any blame. Complaints were made about the Warwick taxi service 'not giving satisfaction'. In June, Mr W.A. Anderton's application to operate a taxi stand opposite the Warwick Arms in the High Street was rejected on road safety grounds. By November the complaint was that there were too many taxi ranks in town.

Bibliography and Sources

Primary Sources:

Life on the Home Front (Reader's Digest)

The British Army in WWII (Greenhill Books)

The Home Front Images of War (Marks and Spencer)

The Warwickshire Soldier (*Evening Telegraph* Special)

The Warwickshire Yeomanry (Warwickshire Yeomanry Museum)

Aitken, Leslie, *Massacre on the Road to Dunkirk*

Curzon, L.B., *A Dictionary of Law*

Dawes, Laura, *Fighting Fit*

Fabian, Robert, *Fabian of the Yard*

Ferguson, Norman, *The Second World War: A Miscellany*

Gardiner, Juliet, *The Animals' War*

Gooden, Philip and Lewis, Peter, *The Word at War: World War Two in 100 Phrases*

Hart-Davis, Duff, *Our Land at War*

Howe, David, *Notes on the History of Coten End School, Warwick and Nearby Schools: Part Two*

Hylton, Stuart, *Their Darkest Hour*

Jones, Steve, *When the Lights Went Down*

Kramer, Ann, *Conscientious Objectors of the Second World War*

Levine, Joshua, *The Secret History of the Blitz*

Lynn, Dame Vera, *We'll Meet Again*

Mackay, Robert, *Half the Battle*

Nelson, Sam, *The Biographic Story of Sam Nelson*

Nicol, Patricia, *Sucking Eggs*

Opie, Robert, *The Wartime Scrapbook: On the Home Front 1939 to 1945*

Patten OBE, Marguerite, *Feeding the Nation*

Powell, James, Sutherland, Graham and Gardner, Terence, *Policing Warwickshire*

Rommelaere, Guy, *May 1940 in Flanders: The Forgotten Massacre*

Rowberry, Roy, *We You Salute*

Smith, Mark, *The History of the Royal Warwickshire Regiment*

Sutherland, Graham, *Bloody British History: Warwick*

— *Warwick in the Great War*

Thomas, Donald, *An Underworld at War*

Way, Twigs, *Dig for Victory: The Wartime Garden*

Secondary Sources:

Leamington Library

The Warwickshire Constabulary History Society

Warwick and Warwickshire Advertiser

Warwick Arms Hotel

Warwick Borough Council Minutes

Warwick Castle

Warwick Visitor Centre

Warwickshire County Records Office

Warwickshire Yeomanry Museum

Individual Sources:

Terry Adkins

John Ashbourne

Tony Atkins

Graham Doughty

John Flaherty

Sam Nelson

Graham Suggett

David Unitt

Gail and Ray Warrington

Pamela Westlake

Philip Wilson

Andy Wing

Index

People

Places – Non Warwick

Places – Warwick